Classic Restaurants

OF

THE REGION

NORTHWEST INDIANA'S ALL-TIME FAVORITE EATS

JANE SIMON AMMESON

AMERICAN PALATE

Published by American Palate
A Division of The History Press
Charleston, SC
www.historypress.com

First published 2021

Manufactured in the United States

ISBN 9781467145664

Library of Congress Control Number: 2021938375

To my parents, Dan and Lorraine Simon, who loved dining out and introduced me to so much of what Northwest Indiana has to offer.
And to Babs Cohen Maza, my elementary school teacher at East Chicago Washington, who I still love messaging on Facebook. I can't imagine having a better teacher. I just hope you don't spot any errors in this book.

The Lighthouse restaurants in Northwest Indiana, such as this one at State Roads 30 and 2 in Valparaiso, also served as navigational tools for small planes and sold gasoline. Unlike any gas stations today, according to a 1930 ad there was dancing until midnight with music by the August Bucci Orchestra. *Steven R. Shook Collection.*

Contents

Acknowledgements

A book like this isn't possible without the hard labor of so many people who love history and work at preserving it as much as, if not more than, I do. There are those I can directly thank and others who toiled at writing about Northwest Indiana, saved slips of history that might have otherwise disappeared or gone unnoticed. After all, who possibly is familiar with the Old Maid's Tavern near Willow Creek in Portage Township that opened in 1836?

Not many, but just enough. Thank goodness.

If it hadn't been for Steve Shook, who grew up in Northwest Indiana and has been instrumental in saving and archiving so many wonderful vintage photos of The Region, this book wouldn't have been possible. Many of the images used in this book were provided by him.

Kenneth Schoon, professor emeritus of Indiana University Northwest and prolific author of books about the many aspects of Northwest Indiana's history, provided wonderful photos and guidance as usual.

Asa Kerr, collections manager at the Porter County Museum, known as PoCo Muse, went deep-diving into old archives, retrieving historic menus and information about the mineral springs that once drew tourists to the Porter County area. Kevin Matthew Pazour, executive director of PoCo Muse, was always there to answer my questions even late at night—on weekends even.

Tori Binelli, museum researcher at the Westchester Township History Museum in Chesterton, also located numerous old menus for me, and Serena

J.P. Johnson & Son advertised the opening of its new restaurant on Lake Michigan. *Calumet Regional Archives, Indiana University Northwest.*

Ard, the museum's curator, was always knowledgeable of local history and so willing to share her deep well of knowledge with me.

Steve Spicer, whose Miller Beach page on his website Spicerweb is full of photos and information, is a valuable source. Steve is also an expert on the Gay Mill, a once popular nightspot in Miller Beach for men and women during the 1920s. Steve has been with me in so many of my books. How can I thank him enough?

Steve Segura, Multimedia Division/ECTV of the city of East Chicago, filled in many, many gaps in my knowledge about local restaurants, and it was a joy to reminisce with him about our lost favorites. Plus, he gave me the pork recipe for the tacos at the now, unfortunately, closed El Patio.

Larry Eggleston, author of *Porter County Lakes and Resorts*, shared his knowledge of the fabulous resorts and hunting camps that once lined the inland lakes of Northwest Indiana and even better, recalled eating at Mrs. Johnson's Chicken, a roadside stop that has become a legend.

Candee Sweet spent hours on the phone with me recounting memories of her father, Al Sweet, a noted pioneering restaurateur who first introduced using credit cards in Indiana restaurants and also featured Chicken-in-the-Rough, an amazing popular technique of cooking now almost totally forgotten.

Angela McCrovitz, the immensely talented chef, restaurateur and photographer, shared her family's history, including a unique dish made by her uncle who owned a restaurant in Gary back in the late 1930s called polenta alla spianatora, or polenta on the table, that can only be found in a few New York restaurants nowadays.

Mike Dosen, who manages the Facebook page "East Chicago in Photos," and all those who belong and answered my pleas for their memories of favorite restaurants still in business and those not—you're the greatest.

I can't thank Mayor Robert Pastrick, as he's passed on, but I'd like to thank his wife, Ruth Ann Pastrick, my former neighbor when I was growing up on Fir Street, as I am sure that she in many ways was the muse for his cookbook, *Bob's Cooks' Tours of East Chicago*.

Thanks to Gayle Faulkner-Kosalko of the Whiting Robertsdale Historical Society for photos and help. The same to Carole L. Cornelison, president, and JoAnn Shafer, board member of the Munster Historical Society.

And to my editor, John Rodrigue, a special thank-you for everything. You helped guide me through this, and I appreciate all your efforts on my behalf.

Introduction

It was either John or Bobby who stopped by Sarti's in East Chicago, but later, Ed couldn't remember whether it was the Kennedy running for president or his younger brother who was campaigning for him. Both were in The Region knocking on doors and stopping in local businesses. You have to forgive Ed, but there were so many famous people who had stopped by his East Chicago tavern. Ed served drinks to John Dillinger before the gangster drove a few miles farther west, where he and his gang shot and killed a cop and robbed the First National Bank of $20,000, and also to mass murderer Richard Speck, who later killed eight student nurses on Chicago's South Side.

John was gone when Bobby returned in 1968. He was the brother running for president this time around, and accompanying him was his mother, Rose, who gave the keynote speech during a large dinner at the Red Lantern Inn, a beach resort on Lake Michigan. Bobby's sisters, Eunice Shriver and Jean Smith, hosted ladies' teas and visited Polish neighborhoods, a delight to the babushka crowd (babushka is a friendly description for women who typically wear head scarves). This act surely would have earned their brother the local ladies' vote.

Amelia Earhart gave a speech in Hammond; ate dinner at the Lyndora Hotel, where she was staying; and talked to her local dinner companions who had run into her outside on the rainy street about what pilots ate on their flights. She finished the evening after too much coffee by drinking a glass of buttermilk to calm her nerves.

Along the Way, a centennial poster commemorating the first one hundred years of the Lincoln Highway. The Merrillville–Ross Township Historical Society Museum commissioned Mitch Markovitz to create this vintage image. *Calumet Regional Archives, Indiana University Northwest.*

Sarti's and the Lyndora were as different as can be. One was a rough bar where merchant marines and millworkers stopped for a drink and often more before and after work; the Lyndora was the hangout of judges and politicians and served rarified French food. But they're both also so Northwest Indiana, a place where cultures, nationalities and cuisine combine.

When our kitchen stove went out halfway through the turkey roasting on Christmas night, we called El Patio and ordered our favorite Mexican foods. My four-year-old daughter came along, and we drove down the dark, snow-covered streets of Indiana Harbor and passed darkened windows of businesses closed for the night. Up ahead, a square of light was all that was bright, the window of El Patio on the thirty-fifth block of Main. Stepping into the soft light, the aromas of chili peppers and adobo sauce wafting through the air, we started walking past the row of retirees who always sat at the counter, drinking coffee and talking to one another in Spanish whenever I was there. Seeing my daughter, one of the men smiled and said something to her, but it wasn't in Spanish or English. At first I couldn't understand, and then I realized he was speaking Korean.

It was a kindly but wasted effort. Nia is Korean, but she joined our family when she was five months old. She didn't speak any other language than English. As for the man who spoke to her, he had emigrated from Mexico to Indiana Harbor to work in the mills, became a citizen and fought in the Korean War. He'd spent two long years there, and the winters were bitterly cold, but he learned the language, he said, as our waitress handed us our bags of food.

Driving home, I watched the patch of light grow smaller and smaller, disappearing because of distance and the swirling snow, and thought about what had just happened. A Korean child with her American mother walked into a Mexican restaurant, and a Mexican immigrant and veteran from a war that had taken place halfway around the world over half a century ago wished us a happy holiday in Korean.

How East Chicago is that?

Called The Region, many of Northwest Indiana's towns and cities are strung along the southern coast of Lake Michigan or at least close enough for freshly caught fish to land on tables of fish joints and swank joints as well. The once booming steel mills created an ethnic jumble of people from Western and Eastern Europe, Mexico, Puerto Rico and African Americans coming north during the Great Black Migration of the 1920s. They worked alongside one another in the mills, intermarried and shared their foodways. If you know The Region, it's no surprise that the owner

NATIONALLY KNOWN FOR GOOD FRIED CHICKEN

TEIBEL'S
½ CHICKEN 65¢

ON U. S. 41. AT U. S. 30 JUNCTION, SCHERERVILLE—2 MILES EAST OF DYER, IND   C-387

Teibel's in Schererville opened in 1926, serving Mother Teibel's fried chicken made from the recipe she brought with her from Austria. *Steven R. Shook Collection.*

of a popular pierogi restaurant hailed from Michoacán, Mexico. It's that kind of place.

The Region was always more about Chicago than Indiana, where the food often takes on a more southern style. Indeed, it always had Chicago's city sensibility and urban vibes, sharing a love of many dishes rarely found anywhere else.

Shrimp de Jonghe—shrimp dotted with butter, bread crumbs and garlic—originated on the South Side of Chicago in the 1890s, when Henri de Jonghe, a Belgian immigrant, introduced the dish at his restaurant de Jonghe's. The restaurant was raided and shut down during Prohibition, but the dish remains a Chicago and Northwest Indiana specialty—and hard to find anywhere else.

Frog legs were in such demand that Vogel's, one of the "perch palaces" specializing in fresh fish scooped up from Lake Michigan in Whiting and Robertsdale just across the state line from Chicago, raised them in Lake George just behind the restaurant. Most of the perch palaces are now closed, but frog legs and perch can be found in bars such as Chuck and Irene's and upscale restaurants like Teibel's and places in between.

Chicken Vesuvio, a hearty chicken dish with garlic, peas, potatoes, olive oil, white wine and oregano that's cooked until it's crisp, most likely originated in the 1920s at the Vesuvio restaurant in Chicago, and it remains a classic there and in The Region at restaurants such as the sophisticated Café Borgia, with several locations, and such old-time pizzerias as the Original John's Pizza in Munster (founded by a Sicilian immigrant in 1943) and House of Pizza (1954). Oh, and did we mention they both have perch on their menus as well?

That's so Region, and so are carne asada; crisp-edged burgers; latkes; Italian beef sandwiches with pepperoncini; sarma; stromboli sandwiches; gyros; corned beef on rye with mustard; thin-crust pizzas with gooey, stringy mozzarella cheese where the centers are cut into squares; pan-fried chicken; and ribs. Sure, some of these are on menus throughout the United States, but we guarantee they're not as good elsewhere.

I never ate at a fast-food restaurant growing up, unless you count Broadway Shrimp in Indiana Harbor, where you ordered shrimp fried to a golden brown and then poured into white bags ready to go. Or maybe Los Burritos, where sopes and tacos dorados were wrapped tightly in tinfoil to be taken to the park or home. That's the kind of fast food we knew. Sure, we'd driven past McDonald's and Pizza Huts in other towns, but why would we even think of eating there? We had our favorite burger joints, like Miner-Dunn and Schoop's, and Italian places like Ono's in Miller Beach, where the owners tossed pizza dough in the air, moving it around rapidly to make

A bus stop with a fountain? Barboul's Greyhound Post Stop was just such a place. *Steven R. Shook Collection.*

a perfect circle, pouring a pool of rich sauce simmering in a large pot on the stove in the center and then topped with cheese and Italian sausage from the deli down the street, scooped up with a large paddle and slid into a five-hundred-degree oven. This was no assembly line pizza where the dough goes in at one end and comes out a fully cooked pizza through a machine—but with little taste or flavor compared to what we ordered at Flamingo Pizza, Miller Beach Pizza next to the historic train depot, House of Pizza or John's Original Pizza.

Almost every year comes news that one or more of the landmark restaurants I loved has closed. Margaret's Geneva House, El Patio, San Remo, Wishing Well, Old Style Inn, Palm Grove and Miller Bakery Café are just a few.

There were others known to the generations before me. I remember my mother donning a green shantung silk sheath and golden earrings and her double-strand pearl necklace on nights they went to the Red Lantern Inn in Beverly Shores. I can imagine them sitting there, drinking a martini (my dad) and a Manhattan (my mom) while enjoying the view of Lake Michigan. The restaurant and building are gone, and the land now is part of the Indiana Dunes National Park. The same is true for another Beverly Shores eatery also on the lake, the delightfully named Greco Casa Del Lago owned by Joseph Greco.

But the story of the Red Lantern doesn't end in the duneland. In 1947, Roger Larson founded Roger's Chow Mein in Minneapolis, which became a successful chain. Larson moved his family to Beverly Shores to run the Red Lantern, and his sons Kenny and David would later run the place until 1986, when it closed. Kenny, who had attended Purdue University, earned the nickname the "Lafayette Hammer" after winning the 1981 Golden Gloves Tournament in Indianapolis. Over time, the Lafayette dropped, the Red Lantern shut and Kenny ended up owning Hammer's on Route 20 in Michigan City, which is still in business.

I was fascinated by places whose doors had been shut long before I was born but must have been remarkable in their day. Barboul's and Nu-Joy, examples of Streamline Moderne architecture, were Greyhound Post Houses (read: bus stations), serving as models of how the company wanted to be perceived—sleek, progressive and technologically driven. The Barboul was particularly swanky, with a flowing fountain out front, a menu featuring steak dinners and a specialty cocktail called, appropriately enough, The Greyhound—grapefruit mixed with gin or vodka on the rocks. Add salt around the rim and you had a Salty Dog—get the joke, hound/dog.

I never was among the crowd who waited outside in their cars after church on Sunday for a table at Mrs. Johnson's Chicken, a place advertising what it must have thought was a big-time selling point—no men in the kitchen. I talked to a customer who remembered dining there as a kid some seventy years ago. He still missed the great fried chicken and mashed potatoes Mrs. Johnson and her two daughters turned out.

I didn't arrive by stagecoach at the Brass Tavern (later the Stallbohm Inn), sit in front of the large fireplace and sip the raspberry cordial made from the delicate red berries growing on the property. Or run up from the shore, sandy feet and wet hair, to Johnson's Inn and order the freshly caught and cooked fish. I didn't take the waters at Knott's Mineral Springs in Chesterton, but I've driven down what's left of the road that led there—the name Mineral Springs is on the street signs.

I never will visit them, as those only exist, if at all, in faded photos, old newspaper clippings, stories someone once told or a battered menu. Maybe the buildings are still there, maybe not, but their stories, if you're willing to go through reams of old newspapers and archives of historic photos, still exist.

I read and heard stories about places long ago that are now just wisps of memories along with those open well before I was born that have quietly been serving meals, some for almost a decade or even more. Those remaining open portals to the past. A step into the Franklin House transports you to 1857, the year James Buchanan was elected president and four before the Civil War started. Drive up to Johnsen's Blue Top Drive-In and you're immersed in Googie, a little-known 1930s (though it really boomed post–World War II) California architectural style not much known in this state. An offshoot of Streamline Moderne, many of its components like large sheets of glass, sharp angles, neon and tilted rooflines can be seen in the Blue Top's design. At Freddy's SteakHouse, it's not vintage or pretend. Instead, Freddy's was swank long before *Mad Men* ran on TV. Schoop's and Miner-Dunn started flipping burgers before national hamburger chains swept aside the ma-and-pa places in a tsunami-like wipeout. But these two still flip away. From the industrial environs of East Chicago, step into Casa Blanca with its flowing fountains, matador posters from actual events and Mexican hacienda interior. At Teibel's, enjoy the pan-fried chicken just as Mrs. Teibel made it for her very first customers almost a century ago.

Treat this book as both a history and a guidebook. The Region is a culinary treasure chest for those ready to explore; each new street might lead to a different country, a different era and assuredly a different dining experience—one that you'll surely enjoy.

Chapter 1

Stagecoach Stops, Railroad Inns and Early Hostelries

Marie Bailly's cooking usually won raves, but in 1831, a group of travelers from Philadelphia arrived by stage at Bailly's Trading Post to find there was no food at all. Tired and hungry, one passenger solved the problem by shooting a blackbird, which Marie cooked and served with cranberries and some coffee. Later, the Baillys provided their guests with whiskey as well. Despite the spirits, years later they still complained about the experience.

Think of stagecoach stops as diners, early settler style. Hungry passengers could feast—if they were lucky—or just try to swallow down what was placed in front of them, depending on the skill of the cook, how well they stocked their pantry and what was in season. Year-round, there would be, depending on the skill of whoever did the hunting in the family, game and fish. That could include beaver, raccoon (said to be one of Abe Lincoln's favorites when growing up), muskrat, venison, hare, wild turkey and squirrel, which was often fried like chicken.

Bailly's, a complex of nine buildings including a stagecoach inn, was located near Lake Michigan on the Little Calumet River in Northwest Indiana, an isolated area where few people lived. It was a huge contrast compared to the sections of Indiana on the Ohio and Wabash Rivers where, in towns like Madison, New Albany, Vevay and Rockport, stately mansions built by millionaires towered on ridges overlooking the water. These belonged to families who made their fortunes transporting goods down the Ohio to the Mississippi and on to New Orleans, where they could be shipped anywhere in the East and even as far as Europe. Indeed,

Joseph Bailly, a French Canadian fur trader, established one of the first trading posts in Northwest Indiana. *Calumet Regional Archives, Indiana University Northwest.*

a fun fact is that the brewery in Aurora, Indiana, sold its beer in Germany, not a place lacking in its own breweries.

While Indiana towns and cities in the south were sophisticated and many of the homes had moved beyond log cabins, not so in Northwest Indiana at the time. It was all swales, swamps, bogs, sand and towering sand dunes, almost impenetrable woods, creeks, rivers, oak savannas and even patches of quicksand all abutting Lake Michigan's southern shore. But Marie's husband, Joseph, was savvy and saw the advantages of building their homestead on the northern bank of the Little Calumet River, where the Pottawatomie and Sauk trails merged. Previously a prisoner in Detroit because of his alliance with the British during the War of 1812, he'd been licensed as an American fur trader by Governor William Henry Harrison in 1814. He now was the head fur trader for the Calumet region.

His compound included living quarters for servants, guests, Native Americans and warehouses, as well as a home where he lived with his wife, Marie, a Native American, and their children, several of whom would attend the new university in South Bend called Notre Dame when they were older. The home was impressive, with its hand-wrought iron, oak and wild cherry paneling and wallpaper said to have been imported from England. A wide stretch of landscaped lawn separated the house from the river, and nearby was the racetrack where Bailly trained his pedigreed horses. He kept a sloop docked at Bailly's Harbor on Lake Michigan (now Miller Beach) to run goods to other ports of call on Lake Michigan.

IT'S COMPLICATED

Before stagecoaches, travel was either by horse or on foot, following centuries-old Indian trails. The Northwest Indiana Sac Trail was the major path back then, made of packed dirt running through Illinois, Indiana and Detroit on Lake Huron, with connections to at least sixteen side trails. These stretched as far north as Traverse City, Michigan, and Green Bay, Wisconsin; eastward through Chicago to Rock Island on the Mississippi River; and southward to Vincennes, Indiana, on the Wabash River. Pathways also connected to South Bend and Fort Wayne, Indiana. There were no road signs, but then, did it matter? After all, how many people could read? Or write?

"A plain horse path which is considerably traveled by traders, hunters, and others" is how Henry Schoolcraft, an American geographer, geologist and explorer, described the Sauk Trail in 1820, adding that a stranger could not follow it without the services of a guide due to its numerous side trails.

At the time the Philadelphians arrived at Bailly's, the location was the last stop for those journeying west to Chicago. Today it's only forty-five miles from Bailly's post—now part of the Indiana Dunes National Park—to Fort Dearborn, which stood where Grant Park is now. Then the trip ranged from six hours to six days depending on the conditions of the road.

We don't know how blackbirds and cranberries tasted, but food was surprisingly diverse depending on the time of year. Wild rice and cranberries grew in marshes, and nuts were harvested from groves of walnut trees. These could be stored along with the fall slaughter of farm animals that, along with wild game, were cured, ground for sausages and head cheese or smoked and hung from rafters to keep away mice. Pigs' feet and other parts were pickled in large barrels. Wild fruit, picked at the height of ripeness, was sun-dried to later be made into jams, preserves or pies.

Apples that weren't turned into apple butter by cooking them in a large cauldron over an open fire, pressed into cider or loaded into barrels were commonly buried in a deep hole dug well below the frostline and lined with straw. Root vegetables such as cabbages, turnips, carrots and potatoes were added, as were salted meat and fish. It was important to dig the hole in a spot near a recognizable landmark. There was nothing worse than being hungry and cold while digging hole after hole through snow and dirt to find buried apples and meat to survive. Sometimes the acidity in the soil would result in the meat fermenting, and while we don't know what that tasted like, it was another way to prevent spoilage in an era when food poisoning was common.

By the time winter came along, the menu was limited, and in early spring, potatoes and cabbages—the longest to last—would be withered and blackened. Buried food would be, well, buried food and less than appetizing. Hopefully there would still be freshly caught fish (if the ice weren't so thick it couldn't be broken open) and game—though by then the animals would have been pretty thin from their own lack of food. Flour and cornmeal, if there were any left, might be infested with bugs, but what could you do but pick them out one by one and use the milled grain to whip up cornbread, biscuits and bread?

In the spring, early settlers tapped maple trees and boiled down the sap to a thick golden-brown syrup to use as a sweetener, just like they'd been taught by the friendly Native Americans who lived in Northwest Indiana. There were also fiddlehead greens, ramps (with their garlicky taste and smell) and morel mushrooms to be foraged—again, another thank-you to the Indians.

A.ROGERS CONTINENTAL HOTEL VALPARAISO IND. J.CONN PROPRIETOR

An 1876 engraving of the A. Rogers Continental Hotel, proprietor J. Conn. *Steven R. Shook Collection.*

Summer definitely was the best time for eating. Tables would be laden with any crops the Baillys might have planted—and critters hadn't destroyed—and there would be bartering with Native Americans for foodstuff gathered or grew. Marie and her daughters would have had chickens, hens and even roosters that no longer could perform their duties to fry or stew, as well as fresh eggs to create tasty dishes. Cows would be milked, the cream churned to make butter and early berries turned into jams and pies. But if you're imagining sweet corn and plump chickens fried to a golden crispiness, forget it. Corn back then, before hybridization, was picked while still green, as that was when it was tenderest. Chickens, allowed to free range, were scrawny and tough. But still, the taste of fresh food after a long winter must have been wonderful.

There also would have been chickweeds; hairy bittercress, which, despite its name, is sweet and tender; mushrooms; dandelions; garlic mustard; and other greens. These might have been cooked with any remaining bacon or salt pork from the long winter.

Cooking would have been done in skillets and cauldrons set on iron swings that could easily be positioned about the fire. That alone sounds hazardous, but even more so, women had to worry about their long skirts catching on embers from the burning logs and setting their clothing on fire. Of course, they wore simple clothing compared to the wealthy women in large cities who favored crinolines and wide skirts, as that was the style. According to historydaily.org, popular Bulgarian journalist Petro Slaveykov published a critical article in 1864 reporting that at least 39,927 women worldwide had died from 1850 to 1864 in crinoline-related fires.

Even the plain woolen or cotton dresses could burn, and so pioneer women had to maneuver cooking stews in big cauldrons, frying chickens and baking breads all over an open hearth while looking for loose embers that might cause a blaze. Heaven forbid they should wear pants.

OTHER DANGERS

Welcome to Northwest Indiana, a place where at night the yellowish eyes of bobcats and cougars could be seen as they crept closer to the settlers' dwellings and the howls of wolves cut through the still air. Even the magnificent bald eagles were a danger. Priscilla Carr, who with her husband and family squatted on Lake Michigan (lakefront property was worthless back then), recalled the time she laid her bundled newborn on the beach while she helped cast and haul in nets filled with six-foot sturgeons. Keeping a close eye on her child, she saw an eagle swoop down to grab the infant. Snatching her baby up and holding him close, she managed to fight off the bird. Just another day in Northwest Indiana back then.

In the early 1830s, thrice-weekly stagecoach runs began making their way along the Chicago-Detroit Road, and several more stagecoach inns were established. The Bennett Tavern opened at the mouth of the Grand Calumet River where it flowed into Lake Michigan in Miller Beach. In 1833, Jesse and Jane Morgan and their seven children settled in an area southeast of Coffee Creek and established the Stage House Tavern on the Detroit Road to Fort Dearborn where it crossed Sand and Coffee Creeks—the latter so named when a sack of coffee fell into the water, turning it brown. Their daughter Hannah was the first European girl born in the area.

That fall, Alexis Pravonzy, a Russian immigrant and local schoolteacher, opened a trading post close to what would become Chesterton. We don't

The Kaske House, now the home of the Munster Historical Society and a museum, was built in 1908. *Calumet Regional Archives, Indiana University Northwest.*

know what he served in the way of food, but during one season, he sold eleven barrels of tanglefoot whiskey (now known as moonshine), mostly to Native Americans, resulting in at least one death that came about because of a drunken knife fight. Considering that a typical barrel of whiskey holds fifty-three gallons, we're talking about heavy-duty consumption in a sparsely populated area.

In 1836, Jacob Bigelow opened the Exchange, a large tavern and stage inn with twenty-two rooms; it was the largest lodging place between Chicago and Detroit. Bigelow was president of the Michigan City and Kankakee Railroad Company and one of the developers of City West, a town with a lot of promise and said to be on target to eclipse Michigan City, which at the time was also in a competition of which city would be biggest and best with Chicago. Located on Lake Michigan, City West is one of a long list of "lost towns'" in Northwest Indiana. Within a few years, all that remained were abandoned buildings, some of which disappeared under the drifting sand; others, like the Exchange, were moved. In 1850, the large hotel was placed on skids pulled by teams of oxen and slid over the snow to Coffee Creek, founded in 1834. The same year, Coffee Creek was renamed Calumet, which it would remain for another two decades before being changed to Chesterton. So far that name has stuck.

As for the Exchange, it became the Central House after the move to Chesterton. Four years later, the remaining City West structures were destroyed in a fire. For fifty-eight years, the Central House was Chesterton's primary hotel. When it burned down, the last remnant of City West was gone.

THE GIBSON FAMILY

It almost takes a scorecard to track all the hostelries the Gibson family owned, but we'll give it a try. In 1837, David Gibson built a log inn at the only place where the east–west high ridge intersected with the Old Pike, an Indian trail running from Lake Michigan to the Great Prairies. Now Ridge Road and Columbia Avenue in Merrillville, it was a busy crossroad, and the Gibson Inn catered to all travelers—explorers, soldiers, French fur traders, pioneers with wagons filled with all they would hopefully need to move farther west, Indians traveling along their ancient byways. Stage travel was still fairly new when Gibson owned his inn, and those walking or riding horses were also a common sight.

About the same time that David Gibson opened his inn after paying six dollars for the land, Thomas Gibson and his wife, Anna Maria, were building a large two-story hewn-log building on forty acres of land that would later be part of Gary. There also was a Gibson Station near the Hohman's stage in what is now Hammond.

Many of the early stopping places were fairly basic, but Thomas and Anna Maria's was no such rough-and-tumble place to eat or stay. According to historian Kenneth Schoon, the property was shaded by stately oaks and surrounded by wildflowers. A grapevine swing added to its appeal.

THE GIBSON WOMEN

Thomas died in 1850, leaving Anna Maria with six children to raise and a business to run. She must have been one tough woman because she more than made a go of it. Known as Mother Gibson, her hospitality made the inn one of the most popular taverns in the Calumet region.

Henrietta Combs moved with her family first from Canada, where she was born, to Chicago by way of Detroit in 1846. Four years later, the family

The Stagecoach Inn at 127 North Main in Hebron was built in 1849. It's now part of a museum complex that also includes the Panhandle Depot. *Steven R. Shook Collection.*

was on the move again, settling in Ainsworth Station, where her father traded two horses, a wagon and a harness for forty acres of swampy land. That same year, he also purchased the James Cassidy Inn, located at the toll bridge, and three years later the Brumley Stage House. By then, stagecoach routes crisscrossed through Northwest Indiana.

"Stages ran on a regular schedule like the railroad, so we knew when they would come and watch for them," recalled Henrietta in 1922 when she was an elderly woman. "The driver of the stagecoach always blew a horn before he came in. Father would have horses hitched at the barn or relay station so they could go straight on to Chicago."

Travelers often lunched at the Combs stage house while the horses were being switched. What they ate may be reflected in another of Combs's recollections, that of catching pickerel and black bass in a nearby slough and picking buckets and buckets of huckleberries, all of which we imagine ended up being served to passengers dining at the inn.

Henrietta's family was friendly with many of the Native Americans living in Northwest Indiana. She played with the young children of a woman who helped her mother with housework. Years later, before the Indians had been driven from the area, she ran into a few she knew from her youth. They were cooking a quartered muskrat and yellow hard corn in a big camp kettle. "They dipped the stuff out and ate it with some kind of wooden spoon or gourd," she recalled. When offered some, Combs was too polite to say no, but it turned out that muskrat stew was not for her, mainly because they hadn't used any seasoning at all.

But not everyone was as friendly with the Native Americans as Henrietta. There were complaints of too many Indians at the Bailly homestead. Some may have been Marie's relatives or business partners of Joseph. Still others probably just lived locally and liked to gather to share news and stories. It's interesting that passengers, traveling across lands once belonging to the Indians, complained about having to be near them.

With few people around, many of the early settlers interacted and intermarried with one another. Combs played with the daughters of Joseph and Maria Bailly, and she married Mother Gibson's son Charles in 1860. Later, Charles would open up the Hotel Gibson in Gary.

THE BRASS AND OAK HILL TAVERNS
AND THE STALLBOHM INN

In 1845, David Gibson sold his inn to Allen Brass for $5,000. Brass and his wife, Julia, used the lumber from the log cabin to build a large rectangular two-story inn with rooms upstairs that could accommodate ten to twelve travelers a night. Downstairs, where the family lived, there were two parlors, one used as a bar for men and the other as the dining room. The other rooms included a kitchen, bedroom and pantry. There were no fireplaces, and heat was generated by cast-iron stoves.

Julia Watkins Brass, the daughter of a Revolutionary War soldier, turned out to be as tough as Mother Gibson and also able to attract a large following. She was praised by contemporaries for her "attractable and delectable" meals and, as an added plus, kept a large jar filled with big round sugar cookies she shared with those who stopped by. Though Mother Gibson's husband died, Julia lost hers—at least for a while—when he caught gold fever and headed out west during the gold rush, leaving her with their three young kids, Cecilia, Olive and Oliver, as well as a passel of relatives (it was common for extended families to live together back then). These relatives included Julia's brother and sister-in-law Oliver and Sarah; her mother, Lucy; as well as Alice de Frees, a young German immigrant who helped with the housework. Besides organizing family members, Julia had crops to raise, food to put up and a busy tavern to run.

In 1845, when the Brass Tavern and Inn first opened its doors, the journey from Munster to Chicago took about a day. Now the trip from Ridge Road (Old Pike) and Columbia Avenue (Old Highway) in Munster is less than an hour.

In the 1850s, travelers at the nearby Oak Hill Tavern supped on pheasant, quail and prairie chicken, as well as potatoes, buckwheat cakes topped with maple syrup and bread and butter. Honey was available for sweetening, and beverages were tea, coffee or milk. A meal there cost twenty-five cents; an overnight stay was twice that amount. A glass or two of port was extra.

Decades later, Wilhelmine Stallbohm Kaske—who grew up in what had been the Brass Tavern after her parents, Johann and Wilhemina, purchased the business in 1864—described it as a thriving place where life could not be dull. And it must have been exciting, with travelers arriving from all parts of the United States, Canada and even Europe. Union soldiers would pass through on their way home after suffering wounds or on their way to battle. As always, there would be French fur traders, salesmen, Indians and visiting neighbors. Whether it was around the dinner table or in the parlor, traveler tales would be shared and news from other parts of the country retold. There were evening dinner parties that, according to Wilhelmine, attracted large crowds from miles around. All this would have been enhanced by Wilhelmina's cooking. Unlike many youngsters at that time stuck on remote farms, Wilhelmine must have experienced a social life that would be exciting even today.

The family was certainly industrious, growing hay and oats to feed the horses and vegetables for their guests. While the Stallbohms were at first dependent on travelers bringing news of the world to them, that quickly changed when the inn was hooked up to telegraph wires.

It was the telegraph that relayed the news of the assassination of Abraham Lincoln, an event overwhelming to those who gathered at the inn to hear more about the tragedy. Whether it's true or not, some contemporary accounts had Lincoln and his family swimming at the beach in Whiting. Indeed, when Mary Lincoln thought she saw one of her sons drowning, she ran into the water, almost drowning herself. Anna Konyvesy Neubeiser was said to have plunged in the water to pull the future president's wife from the water, saving her life. It was said that from then on, when Lincoln was in Chicago or passing through Northwest Indiana, he stopped to visit. He also supposedly stayed at the Audubon Hotel in Lake Station, where

The Commercial Hotel in Crown Point was a favorite for automobiles. In 1909, a stock chassis race was held, with the hotel (under management of Mrs. Beers) providing food for thousands. *Steven R. Shook Collection.*

There were numerous hostelries and stagecoach stops owned by members of the Gibson family, who were known for their hospitality. *Author photo.*

he gave a speech while campaigning for the presidency. They're great stories, and we really want to believe both of them, but so far, there are few contemporary accounts substantiating either.

The Commercial Hotel was a favorite of automobilists (as they were called back then), and in 1906, the hotel contracted with the promoters of the Chicago Automobile Dealer's Economy Test to feed eight hundred people on October 12. It was expected that between one hundred and two hundred automobiles would be in the city on that day to ascertain how far various machines could travel on one gallon of gasoline. Crown Point was selected because of its fine racecourse and the excellent system of macadam roads leading in all directions to the city.

THE END OF STAGECOACH TRAVEL
AND STAGECOACH INNS

Bumpy and relatively slow; easily stuck when the roads turned muddy and passengers were expected to get out and help push; amazingly hot and dusty in the summer, coating everyone with a layer of dirt—stagecoaches couldn't compete with trains for speed or comfort. Less comfortable were the new machines called automobiles, and though there were few roads that were any good, they were a sign of the future. By the 1890s, the Stallbohms' business had fallen to the point where they closed the inn. It was a good time to quit for other reasons as well. Johann was in his seventies, which was much older back then than it is now, and running an inn is definitely hard work. After the building was renovated for the family, a fire destroyed it in 1909, but luckily, much of the furniture was saved.

In an article written after the fire, the *Lake County Times* described the inn as a famous landmark with huge fireplaces and good wine, both of which warmed travelers far from home. The writer wrote of the times when farmers heading to Chicago halted there and unhitched their oxen while others rested their horses. Inside, they sat around, telling stories and news and enjoying Wilhelmina's currant cordial made from the fruit growing on their property that her husband then pressed into wine.

The Stallbohms remained, building a two-story American Foursquare frame dwelling. In 1905, Wilhelmine and her husband, Hugo Kaske, moved into the home, where they raised their family and were part of the social fabric of the community. The home is now in the National Register of

Hotel Lake in East Gary also had several other names, including Old Lake Tavern, the Lake Hotel and, early on, the Audubon Hotel, a stop for the Fort Dearborn–Detroit Stagecoach Route during the wet season. *Steven R. Shook Collection.*

Historic Places. Known as Bieker Woods and Heritage Park, it's a house museum run by the Munster Historical Society and contains much of the family furniture that was saved from the fire, including the piano. A bronze historical plaque was donated in 1927 by Julia Watkins Brass.

CHAPTER OF THE DAUGHTERS
OF THE AMERICAN REVOLUTION

In 1986, a door to the last century opened when Wilhelmine Stallbohm Kaske's cookbook and batches of old photos were discovered in a trunk underneath Stallbohm's porch. It contained not only Kaske's family recipes but also those belonging to others who lived in Munster. It is most likely Munster's first community cookbook.

Kaske's recipes are included, along with vintage photos from that time, in a delightful book titled *The Brass Tavern Cookbook: A Collection of Nostalgic Recipes Commemorating the Establishment in 1845 of The Brass Tavern & Inn, the First Permanent Settlement in Munster, Indiana*, compiled by JoAnne Shafer of the Munster Historical Society.

"The oldest recipes are for a baked ham glaze and apple crisp both dating back to 1855," said Shafer, who, with other members of the society, worked on the book for twelve years. It was a time-consuming job to collect recipes and also to test them.

"I tested a majority of the recipes in this cookbook," said Shafer with a laugh. "That's why I went on a diet. We also had volunteer testers."

The testers made notes helpful to modern cooks. For example, Kaske's recipe for biscuits called for the use of sweet milk. The cookbook notes that "sweet milk is usually specified to assure that sour milk is not used." What we would use now, said Shafer, is whole milk.

Besides providing a history of The Region, the cookbook reveals how the foods we eat have both changed (partridge wrapped in vine leaves having been dropped from most menus today) and stayed the same. Don't we all still love sugar cookies just like those who stopped at the Brass Tavern more than 150 years ago? But what's with the partridges? They seem to be on many mid-nineteenth-century menus. "Partridge was actually a bird that came through Munster," said Shafer, noting that a century or so ago, partridge were so common they filled the sky. Calling Munster's bird population amazing, Lance Trusty wrote in *Town on the Ridge* that "eagles, hawks and owls probed the ground and trees for meals. Thousands of quail, prairie chickens, partridge, plover and grouse thrived in dry sections." Now, we'd be hard pressed to find partridges or quail listed on restaurant menus or in the meat section of our local grocery store. And how many readers have eaten a plover or grouse? Not many, we're guessing.

Not all cooks were as talented as Maria Bailly, Mother Gibson, Julia Brass or Wilhelmina Stallbohm. Passengers often were served simple fare, and a meal might consist of salt pork boiled with turnip tops, a warm salad dressed with vinegar and frying pan fat or maybe pork boiled with potatoes served up swimming in butter.

One passenger noted a meal eaten at a stage stop consisted of salted mutton seasoned with an abundance of dirt, while another talked about rancid butter, sour bread, dried beef and bad coffee. Others had better luck with such meals as fried squirrel, wild turkey, cornbread, potatoes, bacon and eggs.

It wasn't only that the food was bad; sometimes the guests' manners were, should we say, somewhat coarse. The meat, including seconds, might be carved with the host's own knife and fork. Some diners helped themselves to butter, stewed onions, salt or potatoes all with their own knives, which they also used for eating.

Lincoln hadn't been elected yet when the Franklin House in Valparaiso first opened as a hotel and restaurant in 1857. It is still in business. *Steven R. Shook Collection.*

Flies were common during the summer and were really bothersome when you were eating, trying to sleep or using the outhouse—a favorite place for flies to hang out. Pest control solutions included hinging two boards together and slathering them with molasses. When enough flies had accumulated, a stick tripped the hinge, causing the boards to crash together and crushing the trapped insects.

A scarcity of cookware in some kitchens meant the same long-handled skillet might be used for frying bacon, eggs and pancakes and making a facsimile of coffee made from roasted rye tea. Also thrown into the same skillet were tea herbs such as mint, sage or the bark of the sassafras tree to steep in water. Ingenious maybe, but you had to have a strong stomach as well.

Where you dined varied depending on the number of people. During the day, bedrooms became dining rooms, and sometimes dinner was served in the kitchen. Often, there were nearby orchards where apples and other fruits were made into ciders. Rye was made from corn and whiskey from barley, and if you were still thirsty, there was homemade beer and wine.

Traveling by stagecoach wasn't cheap either. La Porte and Valparaiso were connected by a stagecoach line from the 1840s to 1870. To travel from one place to the other cost $1.25. Demand was high, and it wasn't unusual for nine people to crowd inside the coach, and braver or more desperate souls climbed on top and held on. Proximity to fellow passengers who didn't bathe frequently if at all, riding atop a bouncing stagecoach and poor sanitary conditions may be reasons why people drank so much back then.

SPEAKING OF BAD FOOD AND
TOO MUCH LIQUOR…

"At an early period, wild game was abundant, such as deer, wild turkeys, grouse, quail, squirrels, and the salt pork of the settler was relieved by frequent feasts procured by the rifle or shot-gun from the forest or prairie," reads a description of a Northwest Indiana get-together recounted by Reverend Robert Beer in *Counties of Lake and Porter, Indiana: Historical and Biographical*, published in 1882. "At a certain dancing party held in a country cabin, an immense dish of squirrels was the chief attraction at supper. Frequent reference to a bottle of corn-juice had rendered host and guests less squeamish than usual, so that an accident by which the dish was upset on the puncheon floor proved to be only a momentary interruption, but a subsequent deposit in it of guano by the poultry roosting overhead proved to be more than they could stand, and supper was forthwith ended in disgust."

Yes, bird poop would end it for me.

GOLD FEVER

In 1842, Jacob Bigelow opened the twenty-two-room California Exchange in Merrillville, probably the largest stage stop and tavern between Chicago and Detroit. Well known throughout the northern part of Indiana, it was the largest in the district.

Business at first was typical of many inns at the time, but the Exchange hit gold when, on January 24, 1848, James Wilson Marshall, a carpenter originally from New Jersey, discovered flakes of gold while mining at Sutter's Mill in California. The gold rush was on, and the Exchange had the good luck of being on one of the roads heading west.

Merrillville, then known as Centerville, was described by one chronicler of the time as "a Garden of Eden because of the rich flora growing

The rather odd-looking World's Fair Saloon. Note the two dogs and the bird, which appears to be either a raven or a hawk. *Steven R. Shook Collection.*

throughout the community. Wolf and deer were familiar sights around the clearings. And wild pigeons almost completely darkened the sky in the month of August."

After the hotel was destroyed by fire in 1912, another hotel was built on the same spot. But there must have been bad luck in the location because it burned down as well.

"When California was opened up there were lines and lines of covered wagons passing our place from early morning until late at night," Mary Vincent told an interviewer in 1922. Vincent's father, John Wood, built a gristmill on the Deep River where she was born. Mills—so common back then that they dotted the banks of rivers and streams—were where farmers brought grain to be ground into flour and cornmeal. While waiting, they often imbibed and passed on the latest gossip. The mill still stands and is in operation, run by the Lake County Parks.

SOUSED HOGS

The barroom at the American Eagle House located on the corner of Franklin and Main in Valparaiso had tables and chairs made by a talented local chairmaker. Its front windows were brushed with a mixture of stale beer and Epsom salts that, when dried, created the look of frosted glass. The effect was to let in a mellow light without letting those walking by see who was inside. But the one thing that owner Abraham Hall thought it lacked was the raspberry brandy sold at the saloon on the east side of the courthouse square that made owners Solomon Cheney and John Herr so popular with lawyers.

Hall was determined to get a barrel of raspberry brandy to sell before the next court term began, and he asked Jake Axe, who hauled merchandise for local businesses, to take him to Michigan City on his next run. He could have taken the stagecoach but didn't want to, he explained to Axe, though he'd pay him the same amount. "I'd rather ride a freight wagon than that crowded stage with women in it," he explained. "A fellow can't even chew tobacco on the stage because there's no place to spit."

The horrors of not being able to spit! It was almost too much for a man to bear. Fortunately, it seems Hall made it to Michigan City without Axe imposing any womanly rules on him. There, the two picked up the barrel of raspberry brandy. But something happened on their way home. Maybe it was that Axe and Hall wanted to ensure they had the best raspberry brandy, or maybe it was just a dull trip. Either way, there was a lot of imbibing as they rode back to Valparaiso. Once they were at the American Eagle, a hole was bored into the barrel and used to remove some of the contents for thirsty customers in the bar. The men, now really inebriated, wandered away from the backyard, maybe to drink with the others, leaving the barrel behind, without a plug inserted into the hole.

Hogs roamed the yard, and well, they call them hogs for a reason. These particular hogs developed a quick hankering for raspberry brandy. We don't know if the lawyers were bigger consumers of the raspberry brandy than the hogs, but sometime after midnight, a strange noise coming from Hall's backyard startled Herr and Cheney awake. Looking out their window, they spied drunken hogs having a great time—for inebriated hogs, that is. By the time the tavern opened in the morning and the barkeep came out with a tin pail to collect more of the brandy for early customers, the barrel was empty, the hogs drunk and the air blue from the stink of it all.

The two-story Stagecoach Inn, built in 1849 by John McCune, was the first frame building to go up in Hebron and its first hotel. A stopping place on

According to historian Steven Shook, the Central House Hotel, built in 1836, was originally located in City West, one of the lost towns of Northwest Indiana. *Steven R. Shook Collection.*

the stagecoach route connecting St. Louis and Detroit, the green-shuttered white inn played a large part in Hebron's role as a hub of transportation as a rest stop, hotel and place to eat for railroad passengers and travelers arriving to hunt and fish in the Grand Kankakee Marsh, an area so rich in wildlife that it attracted sportsmen from all over both the United States, Canada and Europe. That is, until the marsh was drained in the early 1900s.

The inn came to a point in time that can be devastating for historic preservation buffs. With no business, the building could have been abandoned, but instead, it was purchased and used for residential and commercial use. It did get partly cannibalized in the early 1930s when an end of the building was sold to a doctor who used it for building his home. But overall, it was intact when purchased by Louis Alyea, whose son, Sergeant Donald Alyea, died on a bombing mission during World War II. Alyea bought the Stagecoach Inn using the insurance money and military compensation he received following his son's death. He restored the building; collected historic documents, artifacts and photos; and turned it into a museum and community gathering place.

Just behind the museum is the Panhandle Depot, built in 1863 as the station for the Pittsburgh, Cincinnati, Chicago and St. Louis Railroad that ran through town. Also a museum, these two buildings showcase an amazing look at transportation in Northwest Indiana.

HOW TIMES CHANGE

In the 1960s, the three-story home that Honore Gratien Joseph Bailly de Messein built for his second wife, Marie, who was the mother of five of his children, became a restaurant known as the Bailly's Homestead Inn. The menu of the stately mansion, now a National Historic Landmark, went way beyond an impromptu menu of freshly shot blackbird and cranberries, offering such fare as Effie's Own Stewed Plump Chicken. The meal, served family style at a cost of $2.50, included homemade egg noodles, green garden salad, creamy snowflake potatoes, hot rolls and butter and beverages.

There was also Golden Brown Pan Fried or Broiled Tender Chicago, disjointed with Spiced Crabapple for $2.75, and a New York Cut Steak, described as a "Man's Steak, Thick and Juicy, Served with Crisp French Fried Onion Rings," for $4.95.

All entrees included the salad bar with a choice of dressing; a choice of baked Idaho potato with sour cream and chives, golden-brown hashed potatoes or French fried; vegetables; hot rolls, apple butter and butter.

The restaurant is no longer in business, but the Bailly's Homestead is still open for visitors. Just the way it was when the Bailly family owned it. Plan on visiting.

THERE ARE ALWAYS RULES

Though the days of stagecoaches are now just an intriguing footnote in America's history, let's share an amalgam of rules that were posted for riders to obey in the 1800s:

> *Don't shoot from the coach as it may frighten the horses and the cocking of a gun makes nervous people nervous.*
> *If ladies are present, do not point out locations where robberies and murders have been committed.*
> *Don't grumble about food served at stage stops.*
> *Don't discuss religion or politics.*
> *Do what the driver tells you to do.*
> *Get out and walk when the horses are faced with a difficult terrain; push if need be.*
> *Don't flop against those seated next to you when you fall asleep.*
> *Don't imagine for a moment you are going on a picnic; expect annoyance, discomfort and some hardships. If you are disappointed, thank heaven.*

Chapter 2

Resorts and Inland Lakes

As temperatures soared in the summer in the days well before air conditioning, people pulled out a map, circled their destinations, packed steamer trunks and rucksacks, topped off their gas tanks (it was only seven cents a gallon) and piled in their Model Ts, Chevy Roadsters, Overlands and Hudsons. It was vacation time, and what better place to escape the sweltering summer than at one of the many inland lakes in Northwest Indiana?

Men packed dinner jackets, linen suits, straw hats and knickerbockers for the golf course. Women placed their pearl-backed brushes, mirrors and makeup in their travel necessaire ensembles. And, depending on the fashion of the time—and it changed fast—they took along a seaside walking suit made of wool or a belted dress over large bloomers that tightened at the ankles. There were other bathing suit styles between 1880 and 1920, and none of them looked like they'd be either comfortable or good for swimming. Turkish-style bloomers decorated with sailor stripe frills were cute, but they were made of itchy flannel. Trying to swim in one of those most likely put you at risk of sinking like a lead balloon to the bottom of a lake. A little splashing and letting the waves hit you were about the wettest you could get.

Streamliner bloomers that came down mid-calf at least let a girl go swimming without sinking. It took courage to defy the norms, but that's what Australian swimmer Annette Kellerman did. Described as an underwater ballerina because she performed synchronized swimming in diving tanks, when Kellerman arrived here in 1907 and hit the beach in her form-fitting swimsuit that actually showed legs and arms, prudish Americans were

Cottages at Burlington Beach. John McQuiston, who operated steam launches on both Flint and Long Lakes, built the Sheridan Beach Hotel on the east side of Flint Lake on what was called Burlington Beach. *Steven R. Shook Collection.*

aghast. But gals who loved to swim wanted such a suit, even if it meant being hauled off by the police and tossed in jail. And that's what happened. After all, showing bare skin was a jailable offense. But there weren't enough jails to keep women from wearing those suits, and the ridiculous photos of five or six policemen manhandling one woman into a paddy wagon certainly looked silly when they hit the front page of the newspaper.

Laws changed, and women arrived at the large resorts lining the many inland lakes in Porter County ready to swim, flirt, boat, make friends, play volleyball, climb to the top of thirty-foot slides, dive off the dock and plunge into the lake, drink and eat. When it comes to the latter, many resorts held Friday night fish fries, chicken dinners on Sunday evening and picnics on the lawn during lazy days. There was freshly squeezed lemonade to help quench thirst, maybe with a little spike of vodka from someone's flask. And then all would take a break, heading up to their rooms to see how badly they'd burned in the sun, wash up and put on clothes for soft summer evenings. Depending on the resort, choices of where to enjoy a meal could include a vast dining room with screened-in windows overlooking the sloping lawn leading to the water or dining on a structure jutting out over the lake and held up with stilts.

Dancing and music playing afterward, maybe a late-night swim or a walk to some dark corner to steal a few kisses were the perfect endings to a perfect day. On weekends, big-name bands from Chicago came out to entertain; during the week, it might be a local group. It was summer, it was a resort, it was all divine.

In the late 1800s and early to mid-1900s, the resorts swelled with men and women. But years earlier, it had definitely been a man's world. In 1865, Richard Lytle built a fishing camp and home on Flint Lake, as well as a store stocking goods for campers and fishing enthusiasts. An enterprising man, Lytle also rented fishing boats for twenty-five cents a day. In wintertime, he hired ice cutters to saw blocks of ice from the frozen waters and store them in his icehouse, where they were packed in hay to keep from melting when warm weather arrived.

But ice wasn't the only business. Fishing and hunting camps soon dotted the banks of the rivers and lakes as word got out about the abundance of wildlife. If you're thinking tacked-together boards, no windows and just space enough for the men to sleep on the floor, sorry, we're not talking about that.

Some of the places looked like fancy hotels, such as the two-story Kouts Club, with its white pillars connecting the first- and second-floor balconies evincing the look of a southern mansion instead of a place for men to smoke cigars, drink good whiskey and rye and tell fish tales. The work of cleaning guns, loading powder into bullets for the next day's shooting and making sure the rods and reels were in good shape was for the servants who had been brought along and who also cooked and cleaned. That truly was roughing it.

But then again, many of the camps on the Kankakee River didn't belong to just ordinary gents. These were masters of the universe types— wealthy industrialists, professional men, men of letters and others with big pocketbooks.

Camp Milligan, built in 1869 by a group of men from Chicago, was situated in a grove on the Kankakee River. It was an excellent location for sportsmen, as attested to by an entry in the club's record book noting that eight hunters shot 66 snipes and 513 ducks in just a few days. Over the course of one year, E.M. Shaver, who managed the camp, killed 1,100 ducks.

Located near Baum's Bridge on the Kankakee were the Kouts Gun Club, Kouts Fishing Camp, Indianapolis Club, Louisville Gun Club, White House Hunting Club and Pittsburg Club. The latter was owned by Joe and Harry Wainwright, two brothers who owned the Wainwright Brewery in

Hunting and fishing became popular among wealthy city dwellers in the 1870s, and areas like the astoundingly beautiful Kankakee Marsh were popular destinations. *Steven R. Shook Collection.*

Kouts Louisville Gun Club, built in 1875, was one of the hunting lodges near Baum's Bridge. *Steven R. Shook Collection.*

Pittsburgh, which had been established by their great-uncle in the early 1800s. Obviously believing their beer was superior to anything available nearby (despite Chicago's great breweries), they had barrels shipped from Pittsburgh to the Kouts Railroad Station, where it was picked up by wagon and delivered to the club. There, Kouts pioneer Tad Starkey, who took care of the brothers' boats, bottled the beer for the brothers and their guests to drink.

KITCHEN BASICS

Vera Lorenz helped her mother prepare meals for guests on a wood cook stove at the Center View Hotel built in 1907 on Bass Lake, south of Cranberry Point. It was the only way to do any cooking, as there was no electricity. But that wasn't all that made turning out meals difficult. An outdoor hand pump provided water; the iceman delivered blocks of ice several times a week to be used in iceboxes designed to keep perishables from spoiling. At night, with no electricity, kerosene lamps were lit, providing some illumination. Otherwise, this far from anywhere, when all the lights were out and clouds covered the moon and stars, it was very dark indeed. On the third floor, a large room was used as the sleeping quarters for children, with spaces separated by hanging curtains.

There were other lodges, such as the Cumberland Lodge, north of Schneider, and Fogli's, a two-story, twenty-two-room hotel on the banks of the Kankakee in Water Valley that opened at the turn of the twentieth century and was a favorite among Hammond businessmen, who frequently spent weekends there.

Located near the bend of the river where the Diana Club was located, the river waters were so rich in fish that resort owner Ben Fogli caught ninety-seven pickerel in one day, prompting sportsmen to flock to the resort. In case you're wondering why ninety-seven pickerel in a day was such a big deal, these mild-tasting white fish are often also called walleye, a name we're much more familiar with today.

Fogli's was not only a place for fishing but also for hunting. According to an article published in the *Lake County Times* on January 10, 1917, the hotel had one of the finest and largest flocks of ducks in the state; the fowl typically could be found on the banks of the river in front of the hotel.

Ben Fogli was local—indeed, after the hotel closed for business, his three unmarried daughters continued to live there. But the Diana Club next door belonged to a consortium of Chicago sportsmen and was considered one of the richest of the clubs, which is really saying something. When Chicago men leased twenty-three thousand acres on the Kankakee Marsh, Hoosiers filed suit to keep, as one newspaper worded it, "foreign hunters out." The Diana Club was on a particularly lush piece of land, a place where the water was high because of a dike that had been built. Its setting also encompassed, in part, what had once been rich farmland, perfect for wildlife.

The idea of foreigners (who more correctly should be called Chicagoans) preventing native Hoosiers from hunting the best land in their own state—even if they didn't own the land—was galling. No one, it seems, thought about the Native Americans who had once hunted and fished these very lands and waters before being pushed farther west.

The abundance of wild game and fish was amazing. One wealthy Englishman, who'd traveled all over Europe, Canada and the United States, described the Kankakee Marsh as being far superior to any place he'd ever

CLUB HOUSE, BAUM'S BRIDGE, KANKAKEE RIVER, INDIANA

Though in the late 1800s and early 1900s places like the Club House at Baum's Bridge on the Kankakee River were almost exclusively for men, by the 1920s, women, too, had become interested in hunting and fishing. The Kankakee Valley Historical Society is working to preserve its history. *Steven R. Shook Collection.*

hunted before. In the early days, it was indeed a hunters' paradise, filled with foxes, wolves, rabbits, deer, ducks, geese, snipes, mink, raccoons, skunks, squirrels, muskrats, beavers and rabbits. A photo taken in 1910 shows Dick Morehouse and Jess Smith, two local hunters, proudly displaying their catch consisting of 1,400 muskrats, 10 minks, 8 opossums and 8 raccoons.

Two creeks—Sandy Hook and Crooked Creek (the latter so named because of its meandering)—emptied into the Kankakee, and schools of channel catfish, dogfish pickerel, bass, bullheads, carp and buffalo swam in all three waterways. Wildflowers abounded; masses of goldenrod painted swaths of bright yellow, while masses of big bluestem, a variety of anemones in different colors and around two dozen types of asters bloomed in profusion. In the spring, delicate trillium and jack-in-the-pulpit could be spotted in the lowlands.

From summer to fall, foragers could fill up buckets with wild huckleberries, dewberries, raspberries, black caps, currants, elderberries and grapes. Even today, it is breathtakingly beautiful, but it must have been really something back then when it was wilder and the river hadn't been straightened at a loss of over one hundred miles.

Most of the men who frequented the clubs were millionaires in an era when that meant an almost endless pile of money, and they didn't come alone, bringing their servants with them to bake bread or buy it, cook the catch of the day and set the tables for parties with expensive linens, sparkling glasses, silver utensils and china, just like they would have found in their mansions back home. They also supported the local economy by buying (if they didn't bake it themselves) bread from neighbors along with their butter, milk and other foodstuffs. Country folk who lived in the area went night hunting for frogs and sold the legs to the clubmen for a dime a dozen—an exorbitant price, or so the locals thought—that the out-of-towners willingly paid, probably marveling at their good deal of getting fresh frog legs without having to sit in the swamp all night hoping to catch some.

Many of the names of the wealthy are long forgotten, but some are still known more than a century later.

In 1875, Frederick Denton Kent, the son of President Ulysses S. Grant, along with Algernon Sartoris, who was married to the president's daughter, Nellie, became separated from their hunting party. They found their way to Peter Lauer's home, asking for food and lodging.

Civil War general and bestselling author Lew Wallace purchased a narrow strip of land just east of the north landing at Baum's Bridge. That's where he moored his houseboat, the *White Elephant*, and where he supposedly wrote his

SHERIDAN HOTEL, FLINT LAKE, VALPARAISO, IND.

Sheridan Beach Summer Resort on Flint Lake was built in 1905. *Steven R. Shook Collection.*

Entrance to Sheridan Beach Summer Resort, Flint Lake, Valparaiso, Ind.

Sheridan Beach Summer Resort in 1910. Besides water sports, there were plenty of other activities for guests, including picnic grounds, concession stands, a toboggan slide and a roller skating facility. *Steven R. Shook Collection.*

stupendously popular novel *Ben-Hur: A Tale of the Christ*, which was published in 1880 and is still in print today.

After locals helped a boat that had run aground on a sandbar, they were surprised to learn that it belonged to Benjamin Harrison, then a successful politician and attorney who would go on to become president of the United States. Harrison, who was a friend of General Wallace, became a frequent visitor to the area. He also, as the story goes, sent seeds to the men who helped him for two decades in thanks for their assistance.

Wallace, like Harrison, lived in Indiana. Harrison was from Indianapolis, and Wallace traveled from his home in Crawfordsville to where he moored on the Kankakee. We don't know how Harrison got to the Kankakee, but Wallace made the trip in a luxurious stagecoach imported from France.

Sager's, a picturesque artificial lake fed by numerous springs and created when a large dam was erected to store water for churning the wheel at Sager's Mill, was a favorite of students attending Valparaiso University and others for fishing, swimming and boating. Larger than Sager's, from 1865 to 1880, the fishing at McConkey's Pond was said to be better for bass and the pike than those found in the Gulf of Canada.

In winter, after the ice was thick and frozen through, was the time for skating and ice fishing on the lakes. Holes were cut into the ice, and once

SPECKS HOTEL, FLINT LAKE, VALPARAISO, IND.

Flint Lake's resort business first started around 1862, when George Merrill established Burlington Beach, a boating and fishing resort on Flint Lake. *Steven R. Shook Collection.*

fish were hooked, they could be cooked up in a heavy skillet over the fires, which also were a way for people to warm up. Thermoses might contain hot chocolate, cider, rum or whiskey.

Maybe women wanted to get in on the game or were tired of staying home with the kids while the men went off hunting and fishing, but as the nineteenth century progressed, resorts began opening up along the inland lakes. Instead of just gentlemen, these resorts were open to all, though it was understood that "all" meant just Gentiles and Whites. Heaven forbid someone ethnic or of the Jewish religion would try to book a room.

In 1890, Howard Dickover built the Edgewater on the north shore of Flint Lake. John McQuiston, who owned land on the east side of the lake, built the fifty-room Sheridan Beach Hotel in 1905. He sold it the following year to Sigmund Freund from Chicago, who upgraded the place by adding electricity and running water. Twenty-four years later, it was sold again and renamed the Blackhawk Beach Summer Resort. The new owners added such amenities as a toboggan slide, concession stands and a roller-skating rink and also enlarged the picnic area.

A biography of Charles P. Specht described the hotelier as operating at Burlington Beach, "one of the most beautiful summer resorts in northern Indiana, a place where the natural beautify is enhanced by the comforts that modern life demands." This combination, the writer went on to say, was irresistible, and Specht was profiting by the fact that he recognized it and established at Flint Lake a resort of the highest class.

Burlington Beach is the alliterative title of this delightful place, which is situated on the south shore of Flint Lake, three and a half miles from the city of Valparaiso, added the biographer, noting it was easily reached by the interurban line that ran to Chesterton, Indiana. In 1897, it came under the able management of Specht, and since then had steadily increased in popularity.

His place was described as large, airy and comfortable, capable of accommodating thirty-five people. At the dock were twenty boats, available for rowing or fishing. Flint Lake is full of all kinds of the finest fish, and to the weary city worker, it seems like a bit of heaven to come to Burlington Beach and spend two or three weeks in the invigorating air amid such pleasant surroundings. The prices are moderate and within the reach of all, and the beach well deserves the extensive patronage that is accorded to its popular proprietor.

In 1902, the Spechts bought a resort opened in 1865 by George Merrill and soon built another much larger resort to accommodate the overflow of

SAGER'S LAKE, VALPARAISO, IND.—25

A Native American village named Chiqua's Town after a Potawatomi chief who lost his authority in the tribe after supposedly being so soused that he started a fire that caused the death of his wife. The village was in a valley that was dammed to form Sager Lake. *Steven R. Shook Collection.*

guests. Fish fries were held every Friday in the summer at Burlington Beach, and chicken dinners were the featured food on Sunday. They had gimmicks to attract, including a pontoon plane that lifted only about twenty-five feet above the water but was such a novelty back then. There were also hot air balloon rides and a large slide going into the water.

When Specht sold Burlington Beach in 1921, the thirty-two-acre resort had numerous buildings on the property.

Dinners at the posher resorts, where women and men still "dressed" for dinner, most likely would have included such popular dishes as Chicken à la King and Shrimp in Ramekins—shrimp and peas in a cream sauce topped with buttered breadcrumbs and pot pies with chicken or shrimp in a cream sauce with peas. Vichyssoise was also a popular resort dish back then, and though its name certainly sounds French, the pureed leek, potato and creamed soup that's served cold was created at the Ritz-Carlton in New York City in 1917.

Processed foods were still new but quickly gaining in popularity around the turn of century. To make such dishes as Shrimp in Ramekins, the use of canned shrimp was necessary and, unless it was June, canned peas as well.

BLACKHAWK BEACH, FLINT LAKE, VALPARAISO, IND.—18

The bathhouse and dance floor at Blackhawk Beach Resort on Flint Lake in Valparaiso in 1929. Fed by an underground spring, the ninety-eight-acre Flint Lake is one of several lakes in the area. *Steven R. Shook Collection.*

Once foods were out of season, home cooks and chefs at the resorts had to rely on commercial canned goods. But luckily, they were in Indiana, which around the turn of the century was canning central.

In 1899, 1.1 million cans of tomatoes were processed in Indiana, while the nation's total was 4 million. In 1898, the Van Camp Packing Company produced 6 million cans of pork and beans in tomato sauce. Fall Creek Canning Company, located in Pendleton, Indiana, was canning sweet peas around the turn of the century.

Diners at the upscale resorts probably had the option of ordering such trendy dishes (for the time) as beef and Franconia potatoes and puddings such as Yorkshire or creamed chicken pudding. The latter is creamed chicken topped with batter and then baked in the oven. Desserts like sponge cake, pineapple upside down cake and orange fool—another pudding concoction made of eggs, sugar, cream, orange juice and zest stirred over medium heat until thickened—were favorites of the time.

Red chocolate and devil's food cakes also became popular at the turn of the century. Red chocolate was most likely what we think of now as red velvet cake, typically made with buttermilk, vinegar and natural cocoa

According to Larry Eggleston, author of *Porter County Lakes and Resorts*, around 1892 there were reports of a sea serpent on Flint Lake, described as having a long green round body and round face with whiskers. *Steven R. Shook Collection.*

powder that is non–alkali processed. Devil's food is denser, often made with chocolate instead of cocoa. While we typically use red food dye to make red velvet cake, non–alkali processed cocoa also produces a red color, albeit one not nearly as brilliant as food coloring.

During the first few decades of the last century, resorts catering to the less wealthy would have served meals that called for less expensive ingredients such as red flannel hash (corned beef hash with vegetables), hot turkey sandwiches and half a broiled guinea hen.

The kitchens at all the resorts probably turned out Indiana Spaghetti, so called because the red sauce consisted of diced round steak and bacon. Other menu items would have included succotash, fried chicken, baked ham, chicken and dumplings and beef. Common sides were new potatoes, new peas, tomatoes, tossed salads, coleslaw, green beans, baked beans, butter beans and asparagus, all when in season.

For outdoor dining by the water or in picnic areas, the hotels probably filled up hampers with sandwiches, wrapped in wax paper, containing a variety of fillings or what we call salads like curried egg, lobster, cherry, Princess (think chicken salad with walnuts) and Spanish (hard-boiled yolks and shrimp mashed with a mortar and pestle and then mixed with mayonnaise, ketchup

Lassen's set itself apart from the competition with a dining and dancing pavilion built over the water. *Calumet Regional Archives, Indiana University Northwest.*

and some paprika). Sandwiches had just recently become a big thing, and the cookbook titled, appropriately enough, *Mrs. Rorer's Sandwiches* was written by Sarah Tyson Rorer. Published in 1894, it was the first book dedicated solely to sandwiches. But sandwiches weren't the thick stacks of bread and layers of meat, cheese and whatever we eat today. Instead, they often were served on thin slices of bread.

Most resorts were on the American plan, where meals were included in the price of the room. Still, we suppose that sometimes, just for a lark, guests headed into Kouts, where they could eat at places such as Fritz's Tavern until it burned down in 1911 and the Liberty Café with John Ketchmark as proprietor. There was also a restaurant in the basement of the Kouts Inn, though it, too, burned down five years after Fritz's. Ed Rosenbaum ran a restaurant downtown in the 1910s. Fried biscuits spread with butter and apple butter or other jams and jellies were a specialty. If you're wondering what those are, they're just what they sound like—regular biscuits that are deep fried.

Indiana had been growing corn for popping since the time of its earliest European settlers, who were taught the technique by Native Americans. So popcorn was probably one of the snacks served. Today, Indiana is second only to Nebraska in popcorn production, responsible for one-quarter of

The dining room porch at Johnson's Inn on Lake Michigan in Chesterton. *Steven R. Shook Collection.*

Coffin's Shady Beach was a longtime summer destination. *Calumet Regional Archives, Indiana University Northwest.*

the nation's popcorn, according to the USDA. Cretors, a Chicago-based company, patented the first popcorn-making machine. Before then, you put the kernels in a pan and shook it over the fire until they started to pop. Interestingly, Orville Redenbacher was from Valparaiso.

Other snacks that would have been available included Cracker Jack, first introduced at the 1871 World's Fair and sold in boxes in 1896. Candy corn hit the market in 1880. Today, thirty-five million pounds of corn-shaped candy sell every year. Then in 1892 came Oreos, followed a year later by peppermint-flavored Lifesavers.

Owners of small planes might land across the Kankakee River, where a farmer kept a small landing strip, and make their way across the water to Marti's Place at Ramsey's Landing near Hebron. Owned by Marti Klauer and his son Ron, the restaurant was in business for forty years before closing in 2017. It was a casual place; you could dock your boat on the pier in front of the restaurant and go in or sit on the deck to order lake perch, catfish and prime rib. Their garlic salad dressing was so popular they sold it by the bottle. In a real old-fashioned twist, the Klauers kept a database filled with the names of over eighteen thousand patrons. A card went out to all those diners near their birthdays, with an invitation to enjoy a free dinner in celebration.

CEDAR LAKE, AL CAPONE AND DINING UNDER THE STARS

At the height of the area's popularity as a tourist destination, from 1881 to 1930, some fifty resorts nestled the shoreline of the 781-acre Cedar Lake. It all started with Dr. Calvin Lilley, who in 1836 built a stagecoach inn with a store and tavern on a bluff overlooking water on the lake's northeastern shore. His business expenses—besides building and stocking his business— were a fifteen-dollar liquor license and another five dollars to sell dry goods as well as domestic and foreign groceries. In 1877, Nancy and George Binyon built a hotel that offered swimming, boating, dining, dancing and, in the winter, ice skating.

Ice, it turns out, was big business, and in the late 1800s, companies like Oscar Meyer and Armour Bros. were among those harvesting ice from the lake to use in shipping their meat products in warm weather. At one point, sixty railroad carloads of ice were being shipped to Chicago every day.

The Lassen Resort. *Calumet Regional Archives, Indiana University Northwest.*

In 1895, Armour built an ice barn for storing ice and a large dormitory for its ice harvesters who were working round-the-clock shifts extracting huge blocks of ice from the frozen lake. "At that rate, it's a wonder Cedar Lake isn't a canyon," wrote Archibald McKinlay IV in his Calumet Roots column that ran in the *Times* for about thirty years and covered the history of The Region.

In 1882, the Monon Railroad, which transported the harvested ice, also started running trains for excursionists coming from Chicago. Some of the passengers were newlyweds, as Cedar Lake was fast becoming a popular spot for honeymooners. By 1900, they had plenty of places to stay, including the Sans Souci Hotel, built by Charles Sigler, who also owned the Sigler House and the Cedar Point Hotel, both high-end hotels each with one hundred rooms. To keep his guests entertained, Sigler offered what most of the resorts did at the time: rowboats, fishing poles, beachfront dining and dancing to the music of popular bands. There was also the Kennedy Hotel, built around 1900. Supposedly the bullet holes drilled into the brick exterior were from a rival gang's attempt to off Chicago gangster Al Capone, who is said to have stayed there.

In 1901, the Lassen family, longtime residents of Cedar Lake, started a ferry service, transporting tourists to resorts and beaches.

Young's Hotel and Restaurant rented boats and served chicken and steak dinners. *Calumet Regional Archives, Indiana University Northwest.*

In 1909, the Cobe Trophy Race, an Indiana auto race covering almost four hundred miles, passed through Cedar Lake several times, with the cars getting up to speeds of nearly 88 miles per hour, though the average was 49.26. The following year, the race was held in Indianapolis and became known as the Indianapolis 500. The Cobe Trophy Race meant even more people discovered the charms of Cedar Lake.

The Lassens, taking advantage of the growing number of vacationers and the demise of the ice industry with the advent of refrigerated railroad cars, bought the Armour dormitory after the company closed down its ice business on Cedar Lake. The family also transported Armour's ice barn from the other side of the lake and dismantled it to use the materials for the front of their new resort. The renovation cost an estimated $100,000, but when they were finished, the T-shaped hotel with sixty-five guest rooms, each with its own private bath, was ready for business in 1919. The restaurant was on a pier jutting out into the lake where diners enjoying fish and chicken dinners could do so as the dark waters transformed into silver by the light of the stars and moon and small waves gently lapped around the wooden pilings. Big bands came from Chicago to play, many of them with well-known musicians. Indeed, the Ted Lewis Orchestra, one of Chicago's most famous jazz bands, played at the resort's grand opening.

Victor's Beach, located on the north shore of Cedar Lake, held Friday fish fries and served steak, chicken and fish dinners, as well as featured dancing and floor shows every night. *Calumet Regional Archives, Indiana University Northwest.*

During the day, guests could swim in the clear waters of Cedar Lake, boat, fish, take a cruise of the lake on the ferry, visit Happy Hollow (now known as Coffin's Beach) with its water slide or maybe learn to perform some steps at Salamon's Dancing School.

But there were other reasons to visit as well. Lake County was known for its authorities' ability to look the other way where liquor was concerned, and because of that, a plethora of speakeasies and soda pop shops abounded. The latter were places to enjoy a Green River or Coca-Cola in the front room or step behind the curtain for something substantially harder. But visitors wouldn't have to worry about going into the town of Cedar Lake to get a drink or find a roadhouse. Some of the resorts weren't averse to selling booze.

The Martinez, said to be the precursor to the Martini, is a concoction of Sweet Tom Gin (a sweeter version than most gins), sweet vermouth, Maraschino and orange bitters that dates back to the late 1800s, and it remained a favorite. In the late 1800s and early 1900s, the Jasmine, which was invented on the West Coast, was a mix of one and a half ounces of gin, three-quarters of an ounce of fresh lemon juice, an ounce of Cointreau and half an ounce of Campari that was shaken with ice and strained into

The Point on Michigan Avenue in Miller Beach. The building still stands. *Ayres Realtors.*

a cocktail glass. Also from out west, the Pisco Punch—pisco, fresh lemon juice, fresh pineapple juice and simple syrup—had been a favorite of miners during the gold rush and survives even today.

As the new century began, there were new favorites such as the Jack Rose, a mix of fresh lemon juice, applejack and grenadine, and the Mayme Taylor, named after a nineteenth-century Broadway star and made with scotch, ginger ale and a lemon peel. Today, we think of grasshoppers as an ice cream drink made with crème de cacao and crème de menthe, but back then, it was just crème de cacao, crème de menthe and heavy cream. Another cocktail, the Last Word, briefly appeared around 1916 and quickly became a favorite until Prohibition and then disappeared for decades. Made with Chartreuse, gin and lime, the drink was like a super powerful gin sour.

Dancing under moonlight, late-night boat rides, Al Capone and bullets and cocktails—it's little wonder that Cedar Lake was also known as Party City.

Chapter 3
Roadside Diners

When Andy and Ben Barboul opted to spend $28,000 on a dining spot located on U.S. Route 30 and Indiana 49 in 1940, the two brothers were already well-established restaurateurs. Twenty-four years earlier, they'd managed the Farmer's restaurant across from the grand Porter County Courthouse before opening the Rainbow Room restaurant five years later. A menu from the Rainbow Room in the 1930s shows that a hot pork, beef and veal loaf sandwich with potatoes and gravy went for thirty cents; a broiled steak à la Rainbow with French fried potatoes would set you back seventy-five cents; and salmon or shrimp salad cost fifty cents. The cheapest thing? Both an egg sandwich and a cheese sandwich cost ten cents each. The breakfast menu included wheat cakes for twenty cents; adding ham and coffee would bring up the cost to forty cents.

The brothers, Greek immigrants, were hardworking strivers and in 1940 sold the Rainbow and built Barboul's. The restaurant, designed in the sleek, symmetrical style known as Streamline Moderne, also had a cascading waterfall/fountain topped with nymphs in front of the regal and colorful décor. Ben Barboul was the chef, in charge of a large kitchen equipped with an oil range said to eliminate problems with smoke. The entire building was heated with gas, and illumination was by fluorescent lighting.

And there was the food. Dinner options included turkey, chicken, seafood and steak. Very nice indeed. But even more so considering Barboul's was also a Greyhound bus terminal. The company, founded in 1914 in Hibling, Minnesota, specialized in stylish and technologically advanced transportation.

Waitresses at the ready at Barboul's Restaurant and Greyhound Post House. *Steven R. Shook Collection.*

The tables are set at Barboul's Restaurant awaiting customers. *Steven R. Shook Collection.*

Barboul's Restaurant and Greyhound Post House opened in Kentland on U.S. 41 in 1940. *Author photo.*

Its vehicles were designed by Raymond Loewy, a French-born American industrial designer known for such designs as the classic Studebaker Avanti and President John F. Kennedy's Air Force One. Architect William S. Arrasmith designed numerous Greyhound stations using Streamline Moderne, a style with Art Deco components that emphasized components of aerodynamic design. Big in the 1930s, the sleek Streamline architecture was recognizable by its long horizontal lines, stylized curves and frequent nautical elements. Greyhound used it as part of its branding, wanting to convey the concept of modernity and stylish, adventuresome travel.

Add to the list of "I can't believe it's a bus station" the Nu-Joy Restaurant and Lounge, located in Kentland at the intersection of U.S. 41 and State Road 24. It was designated by Greyhound executives as their ideal modern terminal, a style they wanted to see replicated across the country.

Nu-Joy reopened in 1929, having previously been a skating rink and dance hall. Also designed in the Streamline Moderne architectural style, the restaurant advertised that it had one of the most beautiful bars in the state, which for some reason was accented with a shelf of books on law. But the drinking was serious because, as the ad read, Nu-Joy served "cocktails made the way you like them." As for the name, that came about when the first owner held a contest asking for name submissions. Theresa Reid, who

The Nu-Joy in Kentland served as a Greyhound bus stop, albeit one with a menu featuring charcoal-broiled chicken, steaks and chops and a bar said to be the best in the state. *Author photo.*

had a bottle of Nu-Jul laxative in her medicine cabinet, substituted Joy for Jul and won.

Whatever we expect of bus station food nowadays—probably stale sandwiches out of a vending machine—Nu-Joy's home-style dinner sounds more than a cut above. In 1939, for $1.10, diners had the option of "Soup or Tomato Juice, Sizzling Tenderloin or Club Steak, Potatoes, Salad, Vegetables, Hot Biscuits and Muffins, Choice of Desserts, Coffee, Tea, Milk, or Iced Tea." By World War II, prices had gone up a bit. A prime rib dinner cost $2.10, $3.30 got you a sixteen-ounce sirloin steak and roast beef would only set you back $1.80.

Over the decades, touring buses for big bands such as Guy Lombardo, Wayne King and Tommy Dorsey stopped by. So did Amelia Earhart. But probably the most famous visitor was John Dillinger. The thing was that the gangster, who had recently been shot dead on July 22, 1934, wasn't there to eat. That wasn't true of the ambulance drivers who were transporting his body to Indianapolis, where he was to be buried at Crown Hill Cemetery. They were hungry and so left the gangster in their vehicle as they dined at the Nu-Joy.

In 1945, fire swept through the restaurant, completely destroying it. Rebuilt in a new location, business continued to thrive, and new additions

Black Cat, a diner and motel in Ainsworth, now part of Hobart. *Steven R. Shook Collection.*

were added over the years. Among the popular menu items in the 1950s was chef Don "Tater" Blankenship's Nu-Joy Tater Burger. It's hard to know why they were such a hot ticket item, as it's described as a cheeseburger topped with grilled onions and thinly shaved tomatoes served on grilled bread. Though you did get to choose what bread you wanted. Maybe this is one of those "you just got to be there" items.

HIGHWAYS AND FOODWAYS

Starting in the early 1950s when President Eisenhower was pushing forward his idea for interstate highways, plans were beginning for a toll road running across the most northern points of the state. And here's where it gets interesting. Greyhound established its Post Houses, places to stop and eat along the toll road, keeping the money close by so to speak. These glass houses, again stylishly designed places, were located inside the Greyhound terminal. Another popular chain, Horne's, also could be found in rest stops along the highway.

At their peak, the two chains combined sold over 275 million meals, and the Post Houses even generated their own signature cocktail, the Greyhound, a mix of grapefruit juice and either gin or vodka served over ice. When the rim was salted, the name changed and it was a Salty Dog.

If Salty Dogs and steak dinners conjure up sophisticated versions of roadside dining, there were plenty of down-home roadhouse places to choose from as well.

Greyhound Bus Line was established in 1921, a time when roads were just beginning to go from dirt and gravel. The change to road construction started earlier, with Henry Ford's invention of the Model T, a car with a price within reach of many Americans. Now they needed roads to travel on. But of the 2.2 million miles of rural roads in America then, only 2.5 percent were considered improved. Improved meant using materials like gravel, stone, sand-clay, brick, shells or oiled earth. Otherwise they were dirt—meaning clouds of dust covering passengers in dry weather. As many cars were open back then, often travelers would dress in canvas or some other heavy material along with facial coverings and hats to repel the dust. Rain and melted snow meant an almost inevitability of getting stuck and having to push the car out of deep slogs of mud. Glamorous?

The Hotel Ritz, in this undated photo, is to the far left and doesn't seem in any way comparable to the Ritz Hotel in New York. Notice Dr. Marsh's office next door. Neither gives you a great feeling. *Calumet Regional Archives, Indiana University Northwest.*

Mrs. Baker's Adventures in Good Eating. *Kenneth Schoon.*

But even more than fun-seeking road trippers, farmers often couldn't get crops to market, and "Get the Farmers Out of the Mud" was a common slogan for better roads. The movement for better roads paused when America entered World War I. But interest started up again after the war, fueled by successful businessmen who had the most to gain. Henry Ford was one, and so was Carl G. Fisher, one of the major investors in the Indianapolis Motor Speedway and manufacturer of the Prest-O-Lite carbide gas headlights then found on most automobiles (replacing what were basically lanterns). They believed that if cars were the future of America, then Americans needed good roads to drive on.

Their idea was to create a transcontinental highway connecting Times Square in New York City to Lincoln Park in San Francisco, a route traversing thirteen states, 128 counties and more than seven hundred villages, towns and cities. And because Fisher was a great marketer and Abraham Lincoln was his hero, it would be named the Lincoln Highway. Fisher and his supporters didn't dream of just any old road, so in 1923, they developed a 1.5-mile stretch of what they called the Ideal Road, running from Calumet Avenue to Janice Lane in Dyer and Schererville in Northwest Indiana.

"The road was made of concrete and had sidewalks, lights, curbs, bridges and culverts," said George Rogge of Gary's Miller Beach area, a former director of the Indiana Lincoln Highway Association. According to Bruce Butgereit, executive director of History Remembered, Inc., a roadside park area and campground also was commissioned for the Ideal Road. Edsel Ford, scion of the car company, offered famed landscape architect Jens Jensen, who helped in the preservation of the Indiana Dunes ecosystem, the then tidy sum of $25,000 for the design.

According to Butgercit, the Ideal Road, the most technologically advanced road at the time, was designed to last about twenty years. "It lasted much longer than that," he says. Because the cost of Jensen's plan grew to $75,000, the park was dropped. A monument dedicated to the Lincoln Highway and to Henry C. Ostermann, an early proponent of the highway, rose in its place. Ostermann was killed in a car accident while driving on it late one night in Tama, Iowa. A monument honoring him and the Lincoln Highway is located in Dyer.

Keeping up the monument continues. Several years ago, the Gibson Woods Chapter of the Wild Ones, an organization that promotes environmentally sound landscaping practices, did plantings in a way that would have met with approval from Jensen. Since Jensen only used native plants in his designs, that's what Gibson Woods Wild Ones did, choosing

Blu Bird Motel Modern Tourist Court at State Roads 6 and 49 in Valparaiso served steaks and chicken. Later, the name was changed to the more modern Blue Bird Motel and Restaurant and advertised homemade pies. *Author photo.*

Pronger's Country Inn was ideally placed on U.S. 41, the main road going south from Chicago that passed through Kentland. *Author photo.*

such natives as Rattlesnake Master, purple coneflowers, wood sedge, wood oats, wild quinine, short aster, Jacob's ladder, arrowwood shrub, witch hazel, ninebark and spice bush.

Better roads meant more people hitting the roads, and the need for restaurants, inns, campgrounds and hotels peaked. "Back then, most people just paid a farmer to park in their field and slept in their car," says Rogge. "The farmer's wife would make them breakfast in the morning, eggs, bacon, biscuits, things like that in the morning for a dollar or so."

That is, if she felt like it. To go beyond spending the night in your car and hoping for a good farm breakfast, roadside diners and tourist cabins started popping up. Sometimes they were next to service stations—a three-in-one stop.

It was an age of independent restaurants, such as Mrs. Johnson Fried Chicken (long gone) and Teibel's (still open), as few chains existed. But there were some.

FROSTED MUGS OF SARSAPARILLA

A&W, the first chain restaurant in the United States, got its start when Roy W. Allen opened a root beer stand in Lodi, California, in 1919. Three years later, he formed a partnership with Frank Wright, who had been a former employee. The two expanded into Sacramento and changed the name to A&W—A for Allen and W for Wright. In 1925, A&W began selling franchises to others, making it the first franchise chain in the country. By the 1970s, A&W had more locations than McDonald's. Of course, that didn't last, but there are still several A&W restaurants in Northwest Indiana.

Interestingly, the menu at A&W was based on an old-fashioned drink originally called sarsaparilla, as it was brewed from the roots of the sassafras tree. If the name sarsaparilla isn't familiar, that's because you didn't grow up watching old cowboy movies where the hero, to show that he was a clean living kind of guy, walks into a saloon and, instead of downing a shot of whiskey, asks for a sarsaparilla. The whiskey guzzlers jeer at him for being a sissy, but when one of the bad guys pulls out a gun, the hero—fortified with sarsaparilla—outdraws him, shooting him dead. The crowd understands that despite the sarsaparilla, this is a real deal cowboy, and he immediately commands respect.

Mace's, known for its barbecue and for the stuffed animal heads bagged by its owner lining the walls, opened in 1925 as a barbecue stand in Hohman and Ridge Road and later morphed into a restaurant in Munster. *Kenneth Schoon.*

Allen had purchased the recipe for the root beer he served from a teetotaling pharmacist/inventor in Arizona who devised the recipe—which remains a secret—out of barks, berries, herbs and spices as a substitute for real beer.

WHITE CASTLE

In 1935, White Castle built one of its gleaming white buildings at the corner of 119th and Indianapolis Avenues in Whiting. It was a prime piece of real estate in this industrial town on Lake Michigan just across the state line from Illinois and the city of Chicago. Labeled #30, it was the thirtieth White Castle in the nation and is still in business close to ninety years later. According to the book *Selling 'Em by the Sack* by David Gerard Hogan, White Castle was the creation of J. Walter Anderson, a grill cook in Wichita, Kansas, who took eighty dollars and opened a small hamburger stand with three stools. Hanging a sign reading "Hamburgers 5 cents," he cooked his burgers on a flat grill in full view of customers. In 1921, Anderson was joined in his business by Billy Ingram, who saw the success of the small hamburger shack as a step to bigger things. With a background in finance, insurance and real estate, Ingram came up with a name and an architectural style—the latter a much smaller approximation of Chicago's historic Water Tower.

This medieval motif was reinforced by using stained-glass windows. The outside was whitewashed (that would change in a few years when they became covered in enamel), and each location was the same size and style—ten by fifteen feet in dimension—with a stainless-steel counter and five stools. The name *White Castle* connoted purity (white) and strength (castle). On the wall of each restaurant were painted the defining slogans of this new chain: "White Castle Hamburgers 5 Cents" and "Buy 'Em by the Sack." Cleanliness was always a major focus, with an emphasis on sanitation. It was reassuring because Upton Sinclair's exposé *The Jungle* had revealed all the horrors of Chicago's meatpacking plants (just a few miles north of Whiting) and had resulted in both the Pure Food and Drugs Act (1906) and the Meat Inspection Act (1906).

At first, the menu was simple: coffee, burgers (no cheese—that came much later) and pie. World War II and the resulting meat and coffee shortages necessitated some menu changes, including the addition of egg sandwiches, which apparently were served only after midnight, as well as grilled cheese and baked beans (who would have thought?). French fries were added as a side dish. And because men were at war, the concept of all male servers and cooks had to be jettisoned, and women (gasp!) started working there.

Ingram aspired to better things for his hamburger joint. He hired Julia Joyce as the company spokeswoman and sent her all over the country with the goal of educating middle-class women about the virtues of White Castle hamburgers. To do so, she quoted research, handed out samples and even helped mothers incorporate White Castle as the main course in their weekly menus. She also sponsored charitable events, and the company was one of the first to establish a family philanthropic foundation to distribute millions to the needy.

Hamburgers themselves were relatively new, and there's quite a debate about their origination. There's some debate, but it appears the beginnings originated in the seaport city of Hamburg, Germany, when sailors brought back the concept of shredded meat. But it was Americans who made the sandwich famous—and profitable—when they introduced it at the St. Louis World's Fair. In 2020, McDonald's was ranked by Revenue as the number-one chain in the United States, with $40.41 billion in sales. Intriguingly, the next most popular chain, while it still does some food, is Starbucks with sales of $21.55. billion. A quick add-up of two other burger places in the top ten for 2020—Wendy's sales numbers at $9.87 billion and Burger King at $10.30 billion—makes it pretty apparent that there sure are a lot of burgers being consumed in the United States each year.

Sauter's Place, circa 1900–1904, at the northwest corner where Stage Road 51 and Ainsworth intersected, just south of the Grand Trunk Railroad tracks. The building had a saloon, blacksmith ship and dance hall. *Ainsworthindiana.blogspot.*

My father would take my brother and me to the White Castle in Whiting. I didn't like their burgers but went for the French fries. The restaurant was just across the highway from Lever Brothers. At this particular Lever Brothers, they manufactured laundry detergent. You might think laundry detergent smells clean or at least inoffensive, but that's not so when it's being processed from who knows what chemicals. That odor mingled with the aroma emanating from the sack of sliders my brother ordered at ten for one dollar—up from the original price back in the 1920s of five cents a burger—was far from pleasant when inhaled from the back seat of a car on a steamy hot summer night.

Early roadside eateries continued to be independently owned, and though burgers would eventually become one of the most popular meals in the United States, when automobile travel first became popular, Northwest Indiana was like most of the country—a place where what people ate depended primarily on their ethnic heritage, religious traditions and what were popular foods of the area. Besides hamburgers, several other universal dishes included fried chicken and barbecued meat.

In 1930, Harland and Claudia Sanders opened a gas station and restaurant in North Corbin, Kentucky, a small town near the foothills of the Appalachian Mountains. At thirteen, Harland had learned to cook from his mother, who had to go back to work after the early death of his father. Sanders knew how to cook chicken, frying it up with his special spice and

Shown in this circa 1950 photo, Mrs. Johnson's Chicken Dinner. There were cabins and a gas station as well. *Steven R. Shook Collection.*

herb recipe in an iron skillet. His success was such that in 1952, he franchised his first Kentucky Fried Chicken store.

But fried chicken had long been part of the culinary landscape of the United States, popular even before America broke off from British rule. The first printed recipe for what we think of as fried chicken appeared in *The Virginia House-Wife*, published in 1824. It was authored by Mary Randolph, a white woman from a slaveholding family who was a distant relative of Thomas Jefferson. But even before that, Hannah Glasse included a recipe for fried chicken in her book *The Art of Cookery Made Plain and Easy*, a British cookbook published in 1747. She doesn't get as much credit as Mary Randolph because her recipe instruction said "to marinate chicken."

It's thought that fried chicken originated in Scotland, where they liked to fry chicken in oil rather than boil it like the English. When Scottish immigrants settled in the South in the 1700s, they brought their method of chicken with them, where it was adapted—and maybe perfected—by Black cooks, many of them slaves.

Wherever it came from, by the early 1900s, fried chicken was popular in Northwest Indiana. In 1929, Martin and Stephen Teibel opened a twelve-seat roadside restaurant at the corner of Route 30 and U.S. 41. The sign on top of the eatery advertised one-half of a fried chicken for sixty-five cents.

Now a full-service restaurant, Teibel's remains family-owned and has expanded and now offers catering services and two event halls and can

Another Lighthouse Barbecue Restaurant, this one at Guthrie, Cline and 140th in Indiana Harbor. *East Chicago Public Library.*

handle events such as weddings for up to six hundred people. But one thing hasn't changed. They continue to fry up their chicken using the same recipe the family brought with them when they emigrated from Austria. Other original menu items include such Northwest Indiana specialties as boned and buttered perch, frog legs and chicken livers.

MRS. JOHNSON'S CHICKEN

Despite its location fifteen miles east of Gary on U.S. Highway 6, a destination way out in Liberty Township in Porter County, Mrs. Johnson's Chicken Dinner attracted crowds from all over willing to wait for hours. Even now, more than fifty years since it closed, people still post about the food on local blogs such as the Jean Shepherd Forum (sheptalks.flicklives. com), described as being for all the serious and not so serious discussion of the works and home of Jean Shepherd, a newspaper columnist who grew up in Hammond, Indiana.

The big thing about Mrs. Johnson's, as one would guess from the name of her restaurant, was fried chicken, though she also served steaks and seafood. It was the place to go for lunch after church on Sunday. In the summer, the wait was not only long but also hot. Air-conditioned cars weren't common back then. The 1940 Packard was the first to offer factory-installed air conditioning, but those were expensive vehicles, unaffordable for the majority of the population. Plus, the A/C units were so large that they took up more than half the trunk space. Only two thousand cars with air conditioning were ordered that year. Indeed, it took until 1969 for over half of all new cars sold to be equipped with A/C. That's one reason why benches were placed outside the restaurant—it gave people a chance to sit somewhere other than their hot cars while waiting for a table to open up.

At least the interior was air conditioned, as advertised on the postcards that noted "it was air conditioned throughout," as well as being a good place to bring the family and offering a home-like atmosphere where "women do all the cooking with the names of Mrs. J.L. Johnson and Mr. and Mrs. H. Brojcki."

We assume from the way it's written that Mr. Brojcki stayed out of the kitchen, leaving it to the women to turn out all that food. Like Teibel's, Mrs. Johnson's was a family affair. Lillie Johnson and her husband, John L. Johnson, owned the restaurant, the cottages out back and the gas station next door. Mrs. H. Brojcki was their daughter Mary.

Congles Restaurant and Lounge in Highland in 1940. *Steven R. Shook Collection.*

"I ate there," recalls Larry Eggleston, a local historian and author of *Porter County Lakes and Resorts*. "There was always a long line. The food, fried chicken and mashed potatoes, was great."

THE CORNER KITCHEN

Mary Schulz, owner of Mary's Corner Kitchen (sometimes spelled Korner Kitchen), liked to say she ran a quiet place. "I don't allow any cussin' and no dirty stories." An Austrian immigrant who came to this country when she was fourteen, she had worked at Ma Johnson's making noodles and pies but quit when she was expected to make eighty-four pies by hand on Saturdays. After that, she managed the kitchen at Barboul's after World War II before opening her own place on U.S. 30 one block west of Road 2, where she specialized in short orders, sandwiches and pies.

It was all about home cooking, and even at age eighty-four, she was getting up at 4:00 a.m. to peel potatoes for mashed French fries and hash browns. But after twenty-seven years, she had turned the pie making over to her daughter Helen Schulz Book.

Another daughter, Jeanette Schulz O'Brien, also worked there. Both daughters had cooked with their mother since Corner Kitchen first opened. For a long time, they opened the restaurant at 6:00 a.m. and didn't close until midnight six days a week. It was a wicked schedule, particularly when you take into consideration that the only people working there were Mary, Jeanette and Helen, along with another assistant. Those were seriously long hours. In deference to Mary being in her eighties, the café's hours were cut back to 6:00 a.m. to 2:00 p.m. Tuesday through Thursday.

At least Mary didn't have far to get to work. Her home and restaurant were in the same building.

Schulz closed her restaurant in 1985, when she was eighty-six, and passed away two years later.

Women's names seemed to be an important draw for homestyle restaurants. Mrs. Baker Adventures in Good Eating was a roadside diner in Munster owned by Ida Baker, who was known for her fried chicken and apple pie. The name "Adventures in Good Eating" is intriguing, as that was the title of the bestseller by Duncan Hines, the noted food writer.

BARBECUE

I don't know why it's surprising to me, but barbecue places were big in Northwest Indiana as far back as the early 1900s. The practice of slow cooking meat over indirect heat is said to have originated in Virginia and North Carolina, where vinegar-based sauces were used, most likely because of the large influx of English settlers who brought along their taste for tart and spicy that originated from their colonization of India. They also, because of their colonization of many Caribbean islands, basted their meats with sauces to keep them tender and juicy.

From there, the taste for barbecue hit South Carolina, where the region's large German and French heritage tweaked the sauce with the addition of mustard. Then it was on to Texas and up north to Memphis, where the sweet, spicy tomato-based barbecue was popular.

So how did barbecue become so popular in Northwest Indiana? It might have been one of the recipes brought along during the Great Black Migration that started in 1917 as Black workers left the South in large numbers, determined to escape prejudice and find better-paying jobs in such mill cities as Gary and East Chicago. Every U.S. census prior to 1910 showed over 90 percent of the African American population lived in the American South. Sixty years later, just over 50 percent still resided in the South.

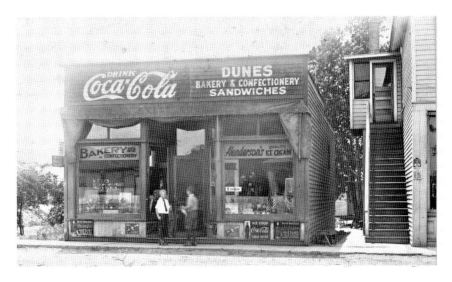

Dunes Bakery and Confectionery in Miller Beach was the place to stop for sandwiches on the way to the beach. *Calumet Regional Archives, Indiana University Northwest.*

Both a strike at U.S. Steel as well as the ongoing Mexican Revolution brought a wave of Mexicans to East Chicago. Their culinary heritage reached even further back when it came to barbecue, as the culinary tradition of barbacoa: cooking meats slowly for long periods of time over hot coals.

It makes sense. After all, Eastern Europeans, who also came in waves to work in the mills, brought their recipes for pierogi, sarmale (the Romanian word for stuffed cabbage) or sarma (the Serbian word for stuffed cabbage), mamaliga (Romanian polenta), burek (a Serbian dish of filo layers filled with spinach, cheese and/or meat) and Polish kielbasa (a type of sausage). And that's just the start. Both the Serbs and the Romanians in East Chicago had their own halls where immigrants could meet, speak their own language, eat the foods of their native countries, dance and drink.

But let's get back to barbecue. The first stretch of paved road connecting Chicago to Michigan City, the Dunes Highway officially opened in 1923. Successful beyond expectations, the highway affected Northwest Indiana both good and bad—no, make that terrible. As the highway made it easier to get to the beaches and resorts in Lake and Porter Counties, the tourism business exploded as some fifty thousand cars per weekend, hauling an estimated 200,000 people to and from beaches and elsewhere, crowded the highway.

According to Arch McKinlay, a newspaper columnist for the *Times* and expert on local history, on Saturdays and Sundays, the Dunes Highway became the most heavily traveled road in the nation. Along with that dubious

Instead of fast-food franchises, the early Dunes Highway, which ran parallel from Chicago through Northwest Indiana, was home to restaurants like Square Deal Barbecue. *Steven R. Shook Collection.*

Located on Dunes Highway, Thad Wilson's started off as a roadside stand and morphed into a swank barbecue place. There was also a Wilson's Motel. *Calumet Regional Archives, Indiana University Northwest.*

honor, so many accidents occurred on the Dunes Highway that it broke the National Safety Council's ghoul counter.

"With Prohibition putting a premium on lawbreaking, after dark was when the road turned into a liquid river of hootch that occasionally got dammed up," writes McKinlay. "Among those who interrupted the flow were the stalwarts of Bugs Moran who not only provided hot competition for the Capone fraternity in Cicero but also gave the Big Guy and his colleagues a series of hot foots on Dunes Highway. After at first standing aside while Capone honored the expensive taste-of-Canada protocol required by Detroit's Purple Gang, Bugs' advance men would greet Capone convoys in the dunes country and lighten their loads." Obviously, there was a lot going on. On the positive side, both gangsters and tourists need to eat.

Thad Wilson owned what in the 1920s and early 1930s was known as Wilson's Barbecue Stand, located on Gleason and the South Shore tracks between Miller Beach and Gary in Aetna. The latter was a company town founded by Aetna Powder Company, a munitions manufacturer, that was later annexed by Gary in 1908. On weekends, Wilson's was the place to go for live music such as Buck Seeley's Band.

But there were some glitches. In July 1934, A.M. Harrman and his wife stopped at Wilson's for lunch while on their way home to 5029 Woodlawn Avenue, Chicago. Sometime during lunch, thieves broke into their machine (that's what they often called cars back then), stealing $500 worth of Mrs. Harrman's jewelry and apparel. That's equivalent to about $1,000 today—worth even more because it happened during the Depression, when a quarter of the population was without a job.

By the 1940s, Wilson's had gone upscale. Now no longer a stand, Wilson's was a sprawling, attractive one-story brick restaurant lined with windows. The menu had expanded as well, serving steaks, chicken dinners, seafood and, of course, barbecue in the spacious dining room. Wilson's also had a cocktail lounge where diners could drink and enjoy live entertainment.

In 1929, Alpheus Americus Williams, a former professor of mathematics and vice president of Valparaiso University, opened the Lighthouse Barbecue and Oil Station No. 10, formerly the Welcome Inn. Situated on the Lincoln Highway and State Road 2 just east of Valparaiso, it was to be charted in an aviation guide soon to be published. Why, you might ask, and the answer is somewhat perplexing but maybe indicative of an early themed restaurant that opened at the wrong time—just as the Depression was kicking into high gear. The Foster Lumber and Coal Company was adding a sixty-three-foot tower to the roof of the restaurant that would be lit by three 2200-watt lights (a special permit was needed for this), making it visible in the air from long distances.

Already there were three other Lighthouse restaurants: in Indiana Harbor at Guthrie and Cline; in St. John, Indiana; and in Glen Ellyn, with two more being planned—one on the Dunes Highway and the other on Dempster Road north of Chicago. The restaurant business had been incorporated a year earlier with a capital stock outlay of $20,000. The incorporators were Lazer W. Saric, Joseph Cavanaugh and William Proehl.

It certainly was a creative idea. Small planes at the time could pretty much come and go as they wanted. Sometimes they landed on the beach amidst sunbathers just for effect.

In October 1929, it was announced that dancing season at the Valparaiso location had commenced. By then, the tower appears to have been up and running, and the interior was decorating in college colors of brown and gold.

The Valpo restaurant attracted regular groups, including the Valparaiso Kiwanians, who in June 1930 held their regular meeting at the Lighthouse Barbecue. On hand was Russell G. East of the agricultural department of the Pennsylvania Railroad, who gave a talk titled "The Geography of the

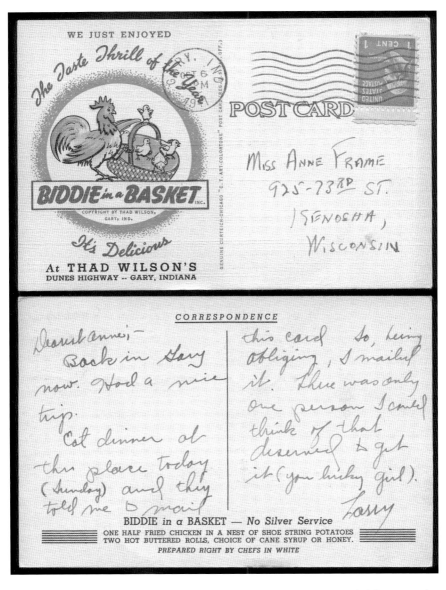

If you wanted to eat on the run, tourists could swing by Thad Wilson's and pick up an order or two of Biddie in a Basket. *Steven R. Shook Collection.*

Dinner Table" at which he pointed out how dependent the American public was on far remote sections of the world for the food and table utensils found on every dinner table. We don't know what the cost of a Kiwanis dinner was, but typically at the Valpo location, cold or hot plate lunches cost $0.50 every

Though it's sadly hard to believe now, at one time, Gary was such an enchanting place that tours were given. *Steven R. Shook Collection.*

Starlight Buffet in Indiana Harbor was one of many buffets in Northwest Indiana in the early 1900s. Most had ads that frequently accentuated the alcohol served rather than the food. *East Chicago Public Library, Calumet Regional Archives, Indiana University Northwest.*

day, but Sunday and barbecue dinners ranged from $0.65 to $1.50. Half of a chicken fry cost $1.00.

The onset of the Depression caused some problems for the little chain of Lighthouse restaurants. On the day before Halloween in 1930, a legal notice appeared in the *Times* that an auction had been scheduled for the following week in order to sell the contents of Lighthouse Barbecue and Oil Station No. 6 on the corner of U.S. 41 and Crown Point Road in St. John, which was in receivership. The auction list was long and gives us an idea of the food served at that location. As far as drink was concerned, there were twelve bottles of Edelweiss beer and one case plus twenty bottles of their ginger ale, as well as eighty cases of Haddon Hall beer, thirty-two bottles of Nehi Pop, seventeen of Hires root beer and forty of Green River, a rather artificially bright green lemon-lime soda pop invented in 1916. There was a time when Green River syrup—that's how they made pop at soda fountains back then—was second only to Coca-Cola. For quite a while, Green River was manufactured by Clover Club Beverages of Chicago and so was popular both there and in Northwest Indiana. Now a nostalgia beverage, it is still served in some Chicagoland restaurants.

Sale items also included thirty-six packages of Old Gold cigarettes, eleven packages of Chesterfields, ten packages of Camels and eight packages of Tip Tops, which were papers used for rolling cigarettes. It wasn't unusual for people to roll their own cigarettes. After all, filters were still relatively unknown until about the mid-1930s, as was menthol.

It's the foodstuff that's most interesting. We tend to think of restaurants of that era serving home-cooked meals. But the Lighthouse inventory consisted of thirteen cans of chili con carne, five cans of tamales, thirty-nine cans of vegetable soup and twenty cans of tomato soup. They also must have used a lot of salt because twenty-six pounds were to be auctioned.

By 1933, the St. John location was up and running again under the name of Warren Wolf's Lighthouse Gas Station Restaurant.

MORE GAS STATIONS AND BARBECUE

At the Square Deal BBQ and Gas Station in Beverly Shores, a lakeside community just beginning to be developed, gas was sixteen cents a gallon, and an open-air stand sold barbecue. There's a house somewhat in the distance between the station and the stand, and according to the description on a circa

NOBLE'S BARBECUE
New Modern Cabins — Fine Foods
Linco Gas Service
On U. S. Highway 6 - 4 miles west junction 6 & 2
and 20 miles east of Gary, Indiana

Noble's Barbecue on U.S. 6, twenty miles east of Gary, featured new modern cabins, fine foods and Linco Gas Service. *Steven R. Shook Collection.*

1929 photo, it belonged to the family of Louis H. Joers, the youngest of four sons of August Joers, grandson of John Joers, who emigrated from Germany and were dairy farmers. It's probably a good guess, since the Joerses owned quite a bit of property and buildings in that location and Louis Joers was the owner of the Dunes Oil Company. The name Square Deal is interesting because Louis was accused of selling bootlegged gas, taking a bribe and not paying taxes, though it all seems to have been settled. And as long as the barbecue was good, we don't really care about anything else.

In 1939, Noble's Barbecue, located on U.S. Highway 6, twenty miles east of Gary in Jackson Township, Porter County, advertised new modern cabins, fine foods and Linco Gas services.

IN TOWN

Kennedy's Tap Room and Grill at 5262 Hohman Avenue in Hammond advertised that the place "seats ten thousand people (21 at a time) and featured Bar-B-Que Ribs."

There was such a high demand for Strongbow Foods that the company started packaging and selling its products. *Steven R. Shook Collection.*

Mace's, owned by Maurice "Mace" Allen and located at the southeast corner of Ridge Road and Calumet Avenue in Munster, opened in 1925. Well known for its barbecue, the place also garnered attention because of Mace's extensive hunting trophies. There are numerous photos of him with his catches in the local newspapers. His wife was also quite the sportsman, hauling in—with the help of her sister—a fifty-four-inch, thirty-seven-pound giant muskellunge. The restaurant burned down in 1952. Later, it became the location of another eatery named The Corner.

Chapter 4

On the Southern Shore

In the 1800s, the beaches along Lake Michigan's southern shore were wild and isolated from the rest of the state. Squatters—often fishing families—set up their shanties and nets, and no one cared if they didn't own the land or pay rent. Wolves still howled at night and eagles soared during the day, sometimes swooping low to the ground in an attempt to snatch babies set on blankets in the sand while their mothers hauled in nets teeming with fish.

But it also offered a plethora of food options. Huge sturgeon swam in vast schools near the shore, wild game populated the area, cranberries grew in the marshes and huckleberries, currants, tiny strawberries and dewberries could be foraged in the dunes. Wealthy businessmen (and they were all men) built luxurious gun clubs where they could spend time hunting and fishing. There were at least four gun clubs in the Gary area: the Miller Gun Club, the Aetna Shooting and Fishing Club, Gary Municipal Gun Club and, the bad boy of gun clubs, the Tolleston Gun Club. Willian Kunert was the superintendent of the 2,300-acre Tolleston Gun Club of Chicago.

There were battles between the poachers and the watchmen who were hired to protect the grounds. According to newspaper accounts, in 1893, James Conroy, head games hunter, and John Cleary were killed by Al Looker at John Harden's saloon. But before you think Looker was just an evil guy, know that Conroy came up to him while he was watching a game of billiards and hit him in the head with brass knuckles, knocking him to the ground, because he had killed a duck when he said he was hunting for muskrat. When Looker got up, Conroy knocked him down again. Drawing his gun,

La Duna was another roadside joint in the Dunelands. *Steven R. Shook Collection.*

Miller Beach Club House, Gary Gun Club, Marquette Park, shown here in 1942, opened a trap shooting range at Marquette Park in Miller Beach in 1936. *Calumet Regional Archives, Indiana University Northwest.*

Looker shot Conroy through the head, killing him instantly. Cleary tried to grab the revolver from Looker, and he, too, was killed. The coroner's inquest ruled self-defense, but Looker fled to Kansas when friends warned him the associates and relatives of the two dead men were out to get him. Good thing too because a few nights later, his father's house was burned down by some of Conroy's friends. So enraged over the killing, Conroy's brother located Looker in Kansas City and, firing from less than ten feet away, attempted to kill him. He missed and a moment later was dead with a bullet in his brain. Again, Looker was let go.

All this violence seems a little overdone given we're talking about a dead duck. But the owners and members of these lodges were serious about their property and wildlife, and there were more murders as well.

The next year, a guard named Dick Stone was killed on the marsh. Another watchman named Lawrence Traeger was shot, but he was lucky because Dr. Senn, Dr. Miller and Dr. Reynolds happened to be out from Chicago, and they attended to him right there in the swamps.

As far as hunting goes, 1894 was one of the greatest years for duck hunting on the marsh. On October 27, F.A. Howe, president of the club, killed 143 ducks, mostly mallards; J.M. Gilispie killed 117; and R.M. Fair, a partner of Marshall Fields, killed 75 green head mallards in the morning and took the

The Hobart House, shown here in 1911, was considered one of the best in town. *Steven R. Shook Collection.*

90

Weidner's Inn on the Dunes Highway, Gary. *Steven R. Shook Collection.*

eleven o'clock train back to Chicago, ducks and all. Kunert went out all day, killing 198 ducks and 2 geese.

But then several things happened that would disrupt, in the long run, the gun clubs and, indeed, the entire wilderness that was the dunes. In the last part of the nineteenth century, sand mining companies began filling train cars with thousands of acres of sand and carting it away, destroying many of the dunes. Entrepreneurs saw the advantage of building steel mills along the shore, and cities like Gary and East Chicago developed into industrial powerhouses.

But transportation works both ways. Even as dunes were being decimated and their sand carried away, passenger trains and electric trains called interurbans began transporting passengers from the Chicago area to the dunes. People wanted out of the city and to enjoy nature, and thus in the early 1900s, there were twenty-two round trips a day between Chicago and South Bend, with stops at seven of the beach towns in between, including Miller Beach and Chesterton, as well as communities that were still unincorporated like Beverly Shores, Waverly Beach, Ogden Dunes and Portage. What had been a wasteland was now a playland.

"In the years before the 1920s," writes Robert Reed in his book *Central Indiana Interurbans*, "one of their major routes began at Hammond and continued on to Indiana Harbor, Gary, East Gary, Garyton, Woodville Junction, Chesterton, Sheridan Beach, Valparaiso, Westville and LaPorte. Variations of the Gary and Interurban Railroad routes commenced at Valparaiso, Chesterton and LaPorte. Typically more than 20 different interurban cars from that line arrived and departed from Gary each day."

Some people were just entranced by the beaches, the dunes and the marshes. Old photos show men in suits and hats walking across narrow logs as they make their way across creeks and women in long dresses traipsing to the top of the dunes. Serious early environmentalists worked at staving off the encroaching steel mills.

As people flocked to the dunes, locals opened restaurants and rented cottages. The Carr family, once squatters on the beach who cast nets into the water to catch fish and then took it by boat to Chicago, built a dance hall, bathhouse, miniature railroad, lakefront cabins, shooting gallery and roller rink on what became known as Carr Beach.

John P. Johnson, one of the many Swedes who settled along the lakeshore, started a commercial fishing business in Waverly in 1907. About ten years

The Carr family turned their fishing operation into a tourist attraction, opening Carr's Bathhouse. *Calumet Regional Archives, Indiana University Northwest.*

The Johnsons, a Swedish family, opened a small beach shack that gained in popularity. It was originally just a beach shack serving fresh fish. *Steven R. Shook Collection.*

later, he and his family opened a ramshackle restaurant. The main menu item? The fish they pulled out of Lake Michigan.

When the state bought Waverly Beach for the new Indiana Dunes State Park in the mid-1920s, the Johnsons moved a quarter mile west and opened another restaurant. That stretch of beach became known as Johnson's Beach. What had been a fish shack now became a complex of buildings. Bill and Elmer Johnson hired Algot Person to build the Johnson Inn at Porter Beach, a thirty-room hotel and restaurant open five months a year.

The fare was twenty-five cents for a jitney ride from Gary to the Gay Mill in Miller Beach, which had opened in the early 1920s. The owners were Thomas Johnson, a Chicago attorney, and his wife, Frances Kennedy, a vaudeville performer who performed at the dance and recreation hall. Located just south of the Grand Calumet River, the place was a huge success and even had a glass dance floor.

In 1927, Gay Mill received a license to operate Gary's first radio station, WKJS—W for the call name, J for Johnson, K for Kennedy and S for son— but it was known by the nickname "Where Joy Kills Sorrow." Performers included an Argentinean guitar player, Bonanova the Spanish baritone, opera singer Fredricka Pickart, Paul Whiteman, Ted Weems, Wayne King

Glass floors, orchestra music, dancing and special transport from Gary and Chicago brought many people to the Gay Mill in the 1920s. *Steve Spicer Collection.*

and a local singing group called the Slag Pocket Four, consisting of employees from the steel mill's Open Hearth.

Also opening was the Dunes White House, a large multistory building with a dance floor, curb service and dining room serving "Sizzling Steaks," as well as chicken and seafood. It lasted well after Gay Mill had closed.

In 1942, an advertisement for "Gary's Finest Dancing & Eating Show Place" proclaimed that it was hosting a New Year's Eve Gala Floor Show with music provided by Bill Funkey and His Band. Prices ranged from $3.50 to $5.00 and included a special eight-course dinner and a bottle of sparkling Burgundy for each guest.

Fifteen years later, the Dunes White House met its end when a fire swept through the building, then owned by Chris Genotos and Gus Callos, causing $30,000 worth of damage.

Dancing, dining and galas were big at Rahutis Gardens, which opened in 1933, but Mr. Rahutis seems to have had legal problems almost from the beginning. He was sued because he didn't pay for the materials used to build his place, was arrested because he didn't apply for a liquor license, a patron sued after being injured by a falling sign and one of his musicians was charged with using slugs in vending machines (a common crime back then). He also lost the Blue Eagle symbol awarded to business owners who engaged in fair labor practices—administered as part of the National Recovery Administration (NRA) established by President Franklin D. Roosevelt—after his waitresses and other staff members complained that he made them work overtime without reimbursing them.

But the Rahutis Gardens, a jazzy, maybe even ostentatious sort of place, remained open, and in 1935, a newspaper advertisement featured a photo of six blondes showing long stretches of bare legs between their short skirts and their white tap dance shoes. They were part of the merrymaking and entertainment promised every night (noise makers and novelties included) and were known as the Six Rahutis Lovelies.

We're not sure what Mrs. Rahutis thought about all these bare-legged and busty blondes running around in abbreviated costumes. But fate was unkind to her. Several years later, she was returning from a Gary beauty parlor after having her hair done for her forty-fourth birthday party being held that evening when she stepped off the interurban and into the path of an oncoming train. All this happened in front of the business she and her husband owned.

If Rahutis Gardens was somewhat tacky, the new Beverly Shores was all about class. Envisioning a stretch of Lake Michigan frontage as the "Atlantic City of the Midwest," Frederick Bartlett, an extremely successful Chicago real estate developer, coined the name Beverly Shores, using the first name of his brother Robert's daughter. To accomplish this, he purchased 3,600 acres on 5.5 miles of Lake Michigan shores.

By 1934, a year after Robert Bartlett purchased his brother's property, sales totals for Beverly Shores reached $1,108,900. And remember, this was the Depression. Sixteen homes were being built, with another five in the works. The landscaping of a botanical garden for the preservation of the rare flora found only in the dunes was completed, as were plantings of rows and rows of poplars and elms along the entire length of Broadway, the main thoroughfare of Beverly Shores, and also the four-mile length on Lake Shore Drive from the Indiana State Dunes and Central Avenue.

Robert Bartlett also moved sixteen structures (four of them by barge) from the 1933–34 Chicago World's Fair to Beverly Shores, including the House of Tomorrow and the Florida Tropical House. Of the original structures, five remain and compose the Century of Progress Architectural District, which, like the Beverly Shores South Shore Railroad Station, is in the National Register of Historic Places. The Spanish Revival style of the depot came to be known as the "Insull style," as it was favored by business magnate Samuel Insull of the South Shore Railroad.

The thirty-two-room Beverly Shores Hotel, circa 1940, was designed by architect Elmer William Marx and opened in 1934. It was a posh place with a botanical garden of native plants. *Steven R. Shook Collection.*

It was, in other words, a posh spot on the lake, with expensive Spanish Revival Colonial– and Mediterranean Revival–style homes topped with burnt red–colored tiles, a country club and an equestrian center. Even the interurban depot (still standing today) fit the theme, with its stucco front and low-pitched red barrel tile roof. Several high-end hotels and restaurants opened up in the area over the years. These include Casa de Lago, a restaurant built in 1930 by Mr. and Mrs. Joseph Greco, and the lovely thirty-two-room Beverly Shores Hotel, which featured a rooftop garden.

Fireproof, the two-story hotel cost $100,000 to build in 1934, featured steel furniture throughout and had a botanical garden conceived of and landscaped by Mrs. Louis Van Hees Young. The gardens radiated from the central pool and had concrete approaches inlaid with colorful tiles designed by Young, who went one step further and baked them herself in the ceramics oven at the Art Institute of Chicago. Young, in case you're not getting the picture, was a noted Chicago art collector who incorporated more than seventy-five plants into her botanical garden at the hotel.

Eighteen years later, the hotel became a nursing home before being torn down by the Indiana Dunes National Lakeshore in the 1970s.

The Pool of Peace in the foreground and the Turtle Bridge in the midground, with the Beverly Shores Hotel in the background. *Steven R. Shook Collection.*

Lenard's Casino was located on Lake Front Drive, west of Broadway in Beverly Shores. *Steven R. Shook Collection.*

Designed by John Lloyd Wright, AIA, the Dunes Arcade Hotel, located left of the Pavilion at Indiana Dunes State Park, overlooked Lake Michigan. *Steven R. Shook Collection.*

Designed by architect John Lloyd Wright, the second-oldest son of famed architect Frank Lloyd Wright, the fifty-room Dunes Arcade Hotel overlooked Lake Michigan. Its spacious and airy dining room overlooked the lake. It, too, like other resorts, was on the American plan.

Lenard's Casino was located on Lake Front Drive, west of Broadway. Constructed in 1935 by the Beverly Shores Construction Company, the first level on the beach had lockers and showers, the second level contained inside dining rooms and an outside refreshment stand and the third level consisted of living quarters. The structure was sandstone and sea-green terra cotta with jet-black trim and was leased by W.J. McCain of Chicago. In 1938, the structure was purchased by Ignatz Lenard (1881–1944), a noted restaurateur who owned the Little Poland Restaurant on 1166 Milwaukee Avenue in Chicago. Lenard later added a hotel wing consisting of thirty-seven single rooms and two apartments. The rooms weren't air conditioned, which was fairly typical for the era in which it was built, and were small, though there were probably wonderful breezes off the lake. The dining room did have air conditioning. Entertainment included an all-girl band on Wednesday nights.

Families frequently returned summer after summer, and one young girl remembered many summers spent there. Meals were included in the weekly

The Red Lantern Inn was located on Lake Michigan. *Kenneth Schoon.*

rate, and she described the family as dining like royalty, noting that she favored deep-fried jumbo shrimp, followed by orange sherbet for dessert.

One of the "famous specialties" at Lenard's International Dining Room were the "Flaming Shashlyk (Caucasian style)." Shashlyks were skewers of meat grilled over an open flame and pretty much sound like shish kabobs, though I'm not sure what "Caucasian style" means. The same goes with another specialty of the house: Filet à la Cracow, for which I can find no recipe even after relentless Googling. But I'm taking it for granted that it was wonderful.

In 1968, the spot in the Indiana Dunes National Park where the casino was located would become the Red Lantern Inn. The sleek Red Lantern Inn, designed by noted Chicago architect Ray Stuermer, featured intimate dining rooms, two lounges, specialty shops and banquet facilities that could host up to five hundred. The dinner menu, provided by the Porter County Museum, was sophisticated. Yes, there was Shrimp de Jonghe, fried chicken, prime rib on Saturday nights and lake perch but also king crab legs, Las Vegas–style stuffed flounder and Beef Kabob en Brochette.

"The first banquet held there was a campaign dinner for presidential candidate Robert Kennedy," writes Kenneth Schoon. "The principal speaker was Kennedy's mother, Rose. The Red Lantern soon became a favorite place for prom dinners, banquets and receptions."

The inn's hotel rooms opened up to a sandy beach on Lake Michigan. In 1986, brothers Dan and Ken Larson, who owned the Red Lantern Inn, having taken it over from their parents when they retired, closed it down. Though they had a lease with the park that was good until 1999, high lake levels and the need for other repairs made any further investment dubious since the park ultimately planned to remove all structures and return the land to its natural state.

Though Troy's doesn't sound Italian, the menu certainly was—featuring pizza pie, lasagna, mostaccioli, baked spaghetti and such sandwiches as Italian beef, Stromboli, Pisano (a combination of beef, melted cheese and sauce) and meatball with green peppers. The lake perch special was Friday night, and one of the desserts was a cannoli.

Over seventy years ago, Josephine Rizzo and her sister Ann Massa opened a little restaurant just off the Marquette Park Beach in Miller Beach, calling it the Beach Box and selling ham sandwiches for twenty-five cents, hot dogs for fifteen cents and cold pop for ten cents. Nine years later, they changed the name to Ono's and Jo's, after their brother Ono Penzato, and added Italian food to their menu. Rizzo's son Sam helped out; though he was only in his teens, he'd already learned to make pizzas from his uncle Tony Rizzo, who owned a restaurant called the Ricochet Tavern in Gary.

The name was well chosen because in 1958, gambler Sam Uzelac was shot in what appeared to be a long-running dispute over the firebombing of a nearby pizza place a few years earlier. The prosecutor called the firebombing an attempt to clear the way for the Ricochet to open for business. This, in turn, led to someone firing shots into the prosecutor's "swank lakefront home."

"In those days, you couldn't open a place without permission from the mob," said Sam Rizzo, who, until it closed for good a few years ago, continued to run the original Ono's and Jo's with his wife, Kathy.

They were a restaurant family. Besides the Ricochet and Jo and Ono's, Josephine and Ann owned Jo and Ann's Food Shop in Lake Station, and the family also owned the Hitching Post, which sold hamburgers and hot dogs in Hobart. Uncle Jack Bianco operated the Pine Grill, a tavern in Gary, until he was shot by a robber. That occurred on August 31, 1970, when two men entered the P&J Liquor Store in Gary that Bianco also owned, shot him dead and took an undetermined amount of money from the cash register.

With all these restaurateurs in the family, Rizzo learned to cook the foods of his Italian ancestors, and he made his pizza dough and sauce from scratch using recipes belonging to his grandmothers Penzato and Rizzo.

"They knew how to cook," said Rizzo. "You gave them a slice of old bread and they'd add garlic and cheese, and you'd have something delicious."

At Ono's and Jo's, one of their signature dishes was the Sicilian, one of Rizzo's grandmother's recipes calling for Italian sausage, imported hot or mild Italian peppers, four different types of cheese and garlic. Also on the menu were sandwiches like Italian sausage, Italian beef, Stromboli and imported ham and cheese, all for take-out or eating outside at the tables in the backyard.

Kathy Rizzo, who grew up in Miller Beach, remembered eating at Ono's and Jo's when young. Though she didn't know how to cook when she and Sam married, she quickly learned.

"I taught her everything," said her husband as she prepared Italian beef sandwiches topped with cheese and accompanied with au jus and a hot spicy giardiniera for two customers—Keith Pollard and Bob Starek.

"I'm fifty-eight years old, and I've had beef sandwiches from around the world," Pollard said at the time. "And these are the best."

Duneland Pizzeria opened in 1972, serving pizza, Stromboli sandwiches and Italian foods, and later became the Duneland House Inn with such items as perch fried to a golden brown. The restaurant served pizza, Italian foods and Stromboli sandwiches.

The Original John's Pizza opened in 1943 when Phil Bacino moved to Chicago from Sicily and opened a pizzeria in Calumet City, Illinois, right across the state line. He later moved his business to Munster, where they have featured not only pizza but also classic Italian dishes such as Region favorites like Chicken Vesuvio, which remains on the menu.

GOOD FOR WHAT AILS YOU: MINERAL SPRINGS

In August 1913, when Indiana governor Samuel M. Ralston ordered two companies of National Guardsmen to set up camp at the Mineral Springs Jockey Club, a racetrack in Porter County, Ben Hyman, owner of the club, boarded a train for Chicago, pausing on the steps into his car long enough to talk to reporters. "I give up," he said. "We can't fight troops. Racing is done."

Hyman blamed the National Commission of Baseball as being behind Ralston's order. "These baseball people, the boys think, have a lot to do with it as the races take away many of the fans," Hyman said. "They have been trying to stop racing all over the country, especially around Chicago."

Hyman also wondered why the governor didn't send troops to French Lick, famous for its racetracks, part of which can still be seen on the grounds of the marvelous West Baden Springs Resort.

The Mineral Springs Jockey Club wasn't the first racetrack in the area. It replaced the Roby Racetrack near the Illinois state line that had been closed down in 1912 amid charges of doped horses and fixed races.

But there was more going on than horse racing in Mineral Springs. According to Porter County History's Facebook page, Armanis F. Knotts built a resort on the banks of the Little Calumet River on land where a mineral spring was located. Naming it Knotts Mineral Springs, he also bottled the springs' water with the resort's name and sold it to guests at his resort and in Chesterton. He was the one who built the ill-fated racetrack.

Knotts Mineral Springs wasn't the first resort boasting the curative properties of mineral water in the area. In 1874, drills bored down eight hundred feet in northeast Porter County near Lake Michigan looking for oil. Instead, they hit an artesian well of alkaline-saline-sulphate water.

Soon, the Carlsbad Mineral Springs Spa and a bathhouse were established, their ads tagging the operation as the "Health Resort of America." It was the era of spas in Indiana, their mineral waters guaranteed

The Norton Hotel opened for business in 1908 and was deemed an instant success. *Calumet Regional Archives, Indiana University Northwest.*

MAIN STREET, HOBART, INDIANA   H-110

The Hobart Café in downtown Hobart. *Steven R. Shook Collection.*

to make the sick well again, turn back the hands of time and, in the case of the most famous Pluto water at French Lick, do what nature couldn't in terms of flushing out the intestinal system for those who were constipated. One sniff of the sulfuric-smelling Pluto water is enough to convince almost anyone of the truth of that.

For a while, the spa, fed by the Blair Artesian Well, flourished, but after the owner died, the new owners failed to keep the clientele happy enough to return.

In 1909, pure spring water from the beautiful mineral springs at Spring Hill in St. John sold for ten cents per gallon or thirty-five cents for five gallons.

In 1922, figures published by the Indiana Department of Conservation showed that the state's mineral spas in business—about twenty-five at the time, including Knott's—brought in a revenue of $500,000. That was a pretty tidy sum back then.

Harry Day opened the Spa, a high-end restaurant, in his old house on Mineral Springs Road on August 3, 1933. Overlooking a winding stream through large windows, its scenic background was matched by the excellence of its cuisine and distinguished décor and accoutrements such as the crystal glassware in the dining room and velvet draperies in the basement cocktail bar. A raging fire destroyed the restaurant in 1951 at a loss estimated at

$200,000, but Day rebuilt the restaurant. Then, in 1959, at age seventy-three and wanting to retire, he sold it. The restaurant stayed in business for almost forty-five years, closing in 2002.

Of all the resorts offering respite from ailments by the taking of waters from mineral springs in the late 1800s and early 1900s, only two survive in Indiana—French Lick and West Baden, luxurious early nineteenth-century resorts that were restored more than a decade ago to their original grandeur. But alas, the ones dotting Northwest Indiana, while still most likely active, no longer are resorts. What remains of Mineral Springs is a road by that name in Porter, part of which runs through the Indiana Dunes National Park.

Chapter 5

Chop Suey, Stuffed Cabbage, Smorgasbords and More

Northwest Indiana is famously known as a melting pot, a coming together of a vibrant amalgam of people from many countries and different cultures, making the area rich in diversity. But what may be surprising to those of us who grew up in The Region is that the first non–English speaking people to move into the Indiana Dunes region and establish settlements didn't arrive from Eastern Europe, Germany or Mexico but were instead Swedish immigrants who first showed up in Chicago in the early 1800s and then began moving eastward into Northern Indiana. Many started farms or businesses in the dune land areas. And, of course, the Swedes were hungry for a taste of home, and stores and restaurants opened that catered to Swedish culinary heritage.

On February 23, 1912, the Lion Store Pure Food Grocery advertised its Lenten specials, including Bismarck Herring and Herring Rolls, each for five cents; and Swedish Anchovies at twelve cents a pound, but there was a catch—you had to purchase an eight-pound pail of the little, somewhat odiferous fish. There was also Oak Brand Smoked Norway Sardines in oil, three cans for twenty-five cents, and packages of Swedish Hardtack Health Bread for eight cents each.

Even those who lived in Indiana Harbor, with its high concentration of Eastern Europeans, Mexicans and Blacks from the South, could purchase limpa bread (a Swedish rye bread with orange zest) and other Scandinavian pastries at Swedish Bakery at 332 Michigan Avenue, which was in business in the 1920s.

Krakowski Buffet in East Chicago. *East Chicago Public Library.*

In 1927, Andrew "Fred" Shallberg and his wife, Minnie, opened a bakery at 528 Broadway in Gary, selling a wide variety of items including potato, butter, egg and limpa breads; Danish butter coffee cakes at thirty cents each; and, in what seemed common in Swedish restaurants back then, Nutty Brown Energy Bread. A few years later, the couple opened another bakery as well as a café a few blocks away at 812 Broadway. Then came Shallberg's Bakery and Shallberg's Pastries, with two locations in Hammond and one in Glendale. They also sold their goods at the Banner Food Store in East Chicago and the Chocolate Shop in Indiana Harbor.

The Swedish Bakery on Franklin Street in Valparaiso was open for decades, selling Swedish sweets. In 1966, the bakery was sold, and the name changed to Henze's Bakery.

Swedish cafés and restaurants would have served the same type of fare as found in the Scandinavian kitchens: lutefisk and potato sausages, smoked and pickled herring, paper-thin pancakes topped with lingonberry sauce and Swedish Press Sylta—a type of head cheese made with pork, veal, allspice and other spices that was a traditional component of smorgasbords. There would have been ostkaka, a cheese mixture with the consistency of a pudding; pfeffernusse, an anise-flavored cookie; and pepparkakor, the thin, crispy cookies made with ginger, cardamom, cloves and cinnamon typically eaten at Christmastime.

Indiana Restaurant in East Chicago is still in business though at a different location than shown here. *Calumet Regional Archives, Indiana University Northwest.*

Johnson's Waverly Beach Lunch Room was the first of several restaurants the Johnsons would open *Steven R. Shook Collection.*

Three generations of Hokansons owned a meat market and eventually a grocery store in Chesterton. During the holiday season, they sold thousands of pounds of potato sausage.

The Chellbergs, Swedish settlers who lived in the dunes and whose farm now is part of the Indiana Dunes National Lakeshore, grew rye for making limpa bread. Others, like the Johnsons—who segued from fishing for a living to catching, cooking and serving fish to guests—lived off the bounty of the water.

But while immigrants enjoyed the foods of their homeland, their children and grandchildren had little interest in eating lutefisk, which is cured with lye. Swedish restaurants and bakeries were disappearing, but intriguingly, they would soon be replaced with another style of Scandinavian dining.

SMORGASBORDS

Introduced at the 1939 World's Fair in New York, smorgasbords became trendy for a while, especially in big cities like New York and Chicago. Northwest Indiana had its share as well.

The concept, originating in sixteenth-century Sweden among the upper and merchant classes, is from *smorgas* meaning sandwich and *bord* meaning table and features butter, cheese, herring, several types of liqueurs, smoked salmon, sausages and cold cuts.

In 1961, Bill and Peggy's Old Mill in Merrillville offered a fish smorgasbord every Friday night from 6:00 to 9:00 p.m. for $1.25 per person.

In 1963, the Smorgasbord at the Fran-Dene Inn on U.S. 30 in the Ainsworth section of Hobart ran from noon until 7:00 p.m. on Sundays. The cost for adults was $2.50 and for children $1.75. The inn, at the time, was under management of Lorraine and Erwalt Major (really his last name was Majorowicz), who also managed several other restaurants in the area.

Featuring fifty-three items, the all-you-can-eat smorgasbord at Walt's Fine Foods on Broad Street in Griffith in 1964 cost $2.75 per person; family groups were invited.

Though you wouldn't expect it from the name, Bud's Lounge on Main Street in Griffith featured a smorgasbord every Friday and Saturday night along with its typical dinner fare of chicken, seafood, steak and the daily businessman's lunch.

Even in little Kouts, Johnny's Corner Tap, formerly Fritz's Tavern, featured a smorgasbord.

In 1989, Baum's Bridge Inn's "gigantic" smorgasbord featured a huge salad and dessert bar, plus peel-and-eat cocktail shrimp, lake perch, split crab legs, frog legs, shark shrimp, cod, halibut, sirloin steak and barbecued ribs, as well as lots, lots more.

BUFFETS

Articles about buffets typically connect their beginnings to the Las Vegas Rat Pack days in the 1950s. But we've got news for them. In Northwest Indiana, buffets date back to the turn of the last century, and there were certainly a number of them, including the Gary Buffet and Restaurant. Owned by Charles Della-Chiess, it was located on Broadway, and—this seems common for buffets back then—not only was it a place to eat, but the focus seemed to be, according to the ads, as purveyors of "only high grade goods—cigars, wines and liquors."

The Borman Buffet, on Broadway and Tenth in Gary, opened in the early 1900s and later became the Borman Drugstore and then later a bank.

McKinney and Jones announced the opening of their new buffet restaurant, described as being the best in the city, in the Lash Hotel in Hammond on August 21, 1908. It must have been a posh place; the fixtures alone cost $30,000.

In East Chicago, there was the rather romantic-sounding Starlight Tavern and Buffet.

In 1907, Kaufmann's New Empire Hotel and Buffet in Indiana Harbor opened for business, advertising a full line of domestic and imported liquors and cigars.

Goldsmith's Café and Buffet in Whiting advertised in 1910 that its chop suey cost twenty-five cents, fish dinners were thirty-five cents and they also served sandwiches of all kinds, as well as steak dinners. There was a buffet at Amazon, a restaurant on Third and Central in Munster.

A Dr. Graham was attacked at Meeker and McCune's Buffet by a thug in Hammond in 1913. It wasn't that type of place, being touted as one of the finest in Hammond. Its gourmand foods included barrels of shrimp imported from New Orleans in 1903. In 1909, they did an expensive remodeling of the building that included extending the bar and placing an art glass canopy over the entrance. Founded around the turn of the century, here's a snippet to give one an idea about how elegant it was.

Left: Blatz seemed to be the beer to drink at the Borman Buffet on Broadway and Tenth in Gary in 1908. *East Chicago Public Library.*

Below: Kaufmann's New Empire Hotel and Buffet opened in Indiana Harbor in 1907 advertising a full line of imported and domestic beers, liquors and cigars. *Regional Archives, Indiana University Northwest.*

It had once been a custom for local saloonkeepers to offer free shots on the afternoon of New Year's Eve, but John McCune and Gus Meeker kicked that tradition up several notches, serving a champagne punch. The ritual began about 4:00 p.m. when a huge glass bowl was set out containing a large cake of ice in which fresh fruit had been frozen. Atop the ice were clusters of Malaga grapes. Lush slices of orange, rich and juicy slices of pineapple, Maraschino cherries and measures of Polonarius water and ginger ale were added, and then the champagne was uncorked and poured into the bowl, then stirred gently. An immaculately dressed bartender used a silver ladle to fill long-stemmed cocktail glasses trimmed with slivers of lime around the rims. Nothing like free booze in a posh atmosphere to get the New Year going.

But posh couldn't keep out the reformers, determined to keep Northwest Indiana residents—as well as those all over the country—from enjoying an alcoholic beverage or two. Meeker was arrested, along with ten other saloon owners, and was the first to go to trial in 1906. The charges were violating the Nicholson Law by keeping the back door of the saloon open on Sundays, an unspoken invitation for customers to come in. I'm sure it was an oversight, and maybe the jury agreed with my way of thinking, because even though Meeker was tried by upright businessmen (remember, women couldn't vote then and so couldn't serve on juries), he was found not guilty. Call it a guess, but it seems likely that some of those jurors found that back door very inviting on Sundays.

Unfortunately, the draconian liquor laws caught up with saloonkeepers everywhere when Prohibition went into effect. Meeker and McCune, known for its quality food and liquor and the geniality of the owners, closed down.

BUFFET, BOOZE, CASH AND BINZEN

Michael Binzen's competitors looked on the Binzenhoff Buffet in Gary as the biggest gold mine in the northern section of the state. But it was one of one hundred saloons or so in Gary that had to close when, in 1909, "wet forces" managed to get a referendum passed that closed down all the city's watering holes. It took a year of being dry—much too long for most—until the law could be reversed.

Binzen was waiting, opening his doors early in the morning once again after the yearlong moratorium on taverns. The timing was perfect, and the

The temperance movement was becoming stronger throughout the United States as religious groups joined with women in broadcasting the negative affect of drinking on moral and family values. *Steven R. Shook Collection.*

place immediately filled up with thirsty millworkers stopping by to get a drink or two on their way to work.

The Binzenhoff was indeed a gold mine, and in 1917, four guys decided to do a little gold digging of their own. It wasn't much of a secret that after closing at night, Binzen walked home with valises full of money from his saloon at Fourth Avenue and Broadway. The amounts at a time were said to be between $75,000 and $100,000 if he hadn't been able to get to the bank during the day. Binzen and Spencer Tillman, his porter who had worked for him for a decade, were carrying that day's cash. The two followed their usual route, past the main gate of the Gary Plant of the Illinois Steel Company and the Gary State Bank. Binzen had his hand on the weapon in his pocket, and Tillman carried a gun in one hand; the other held the money, and another gun was stuck in his pocket.

It was a short walk, or would have been, but after turning onto Sixth Avenue, three men stepped out of a storm cellar four hundred feet or so from the posh Gary Hotel. Witnesses would tell the police that the men

112

The Gary remonstrance was the work of Indiana's Anti-Saloon League and resulted in the closing of more than one hundred bars in the city in 1909. *Calumet Regional Archives, Indiana University Northwest.*

worked fast, one striking Binzen on the head with a lead pipe wrapped in paper. The two other men attacked Tillman. Fighting back, Tillman fired but missed. Two more shots blasted out, with one .38-caliber revolver bullet hitting Tillman in the head and another .38 in the heart. He fell to the ground, already dead. He left a widow.

Taking the money, the robbers ran to the back of the hotel, where an open Ford waited for them. The amount was about $10,000; they missed the $17,000 Binzen had hidden inside his coat. A grocery store delivery man gave chase but then had second thoughts, realizing he didn't have a gun and the others did.

While Binzen was taken to the home of Dr. Templin for treatment, the police split up, some investigating the scene and others hunting for the getaway car. The Gary police asked the East Chicago police for backup, and they arrived, their cars filled with weapons.

Speeding through East Chicago, the robbers made their escape to Chicago. It wasn't until a few months later that Sonny Dunn, on trial for

The ten-story Knights of Columbus Hotel in Gary was built in 1925 at the southeast corner of West Fifth Avenue and Madison Street. *Commonwealth*.

another crime, was recognized by three Gary Hotel employees as one of the attackers. No Boy Scout, Dunn had previously murdered several other people. Despite his record and the identification of the three witnesses, he was so well connected (or mobbed up, as they called it) that a judge turned down Gary's request for extradition.

Binzen recovered and continued running the saloon he owned with his brother. By 1924, when Sonny Dunn was arrested again, he wasn't living in Gary anymore. The local news reported that Dunn had been busted for stealing a basket of meat and a few pennies. Not afraid to gloat, they scoffed at how low this murderer had fallen that he was reduced to purloining pennies and meat. It was justice of sorts.

As an added note about Gary Hotel, Northwest Indiana historian and professor emeritus at Indiana University Northwest James Lane recalled, "Around the turn of the century, I've often heard that when the Hotel Gary was in its golden age, Chicago gangsters would come over and cool their heels at the hotel when things got too hot for them in Illinois."

SCHNITZEL: THE GERMAN INFLUENCE

In 1849, political and religious unrest sent tidal waves of German immigrants to the United States, and for the rest of the century, more and more Germans made their way to this country, with a large number settling in Northwest Indiana in the late 1880s.

Restaurants strictly catering to the tastes of the motherland were popular around the turn of the century, some surviving even longer. Eschenbach's Restaurant and Bakery was located at 707 Chicago Avenue in East Chicago in the early 1900s. There was also Eschenbach's of Chesterton, with the tagline of "Chesterton's Finest Dining and Fountain Service," featuring pan-fried chicken, fried sugar-cured ham and French fried shrimp with Snappy Hot Sauce.

The German Restaurant on Broadway in Gary was looking for a good cook in 1909, and another German restaurant (name unknown) advertised for a waitress in Whiting in 1925. But as non–German Americans began enjoying German fare, other restaurants started adding schnitzel and other items to their menus.

In 1909, a men's club was being built in Hammond with a rathskeller in the basement and a bowling alley on the second floor.

Phil Smidt was known as the Prince of Perch. *Steven R. Shook Collection.*

Fred Dietrich and his sons, Paul, Emil, Charley, Fred Jr. and John, owned and operated Dietrich's Bakery at Truman Street and Calumet Avenue. They were the makers of two popular brands of bread in Hammond—Big Yankee Bread and Cream Bread. A busy place, in 1917, in response to a bakers' strike, they upped the 4,500 loaves of bread they baked a night to 6,000 in order to help with the bread shortage.

On June 30, 1911, an elaborate dinner menu for a Hammond restaurant began with Cream of Asparagus with Toasted Bread Cubes, Weinre (a German spelling of wiener) Schnitzel, Peas in Potato Patties, sliced tomatoes, coffee and Rhubarb Shortcake.

In 1912, Lake Woods Park, "the prettiest park in the west" in Gary, advertised music in its rathskeller.

The Special Table d'hôtel Dinner at the Hammond Café on Sunday, January 14, 1917, cost sixty cents and started with Cream of Chicken Soup with Rice, celery and sweet mixed pickles followed by Baked Cream Salmon à la Merney, Potato Croquettes, Mashed Potatoes, Candied Sweet Potatoes, Asparagus Tips à la Vinaigrette and Queen Fritters Vanilla Sauce for dessert. Coffee was also included. Regarding the Merney sauce, a Google search turned up no matches, but there is a Mornay sauce, which is a cheese and cream concoction that doesn't really sound like it would go well with salmon, but then this was more than a century ago.

But wait, if you thought that was all there was for your sixty cents, there's still the entrée to consume. Diners could choose from the following: Broiled Chicken and Salt Pork with Celery Sauce, Small Beef Tenderloin Steak Creole, Fricassee of Chicken with Noodles, Roast Stuffed Young Chicken with Jelly, Roast Turkey Dressing and Cranberry Sauce, Roast Prime Ribs of Beef au Jus and Paprica (paprika spelled with a *c* instead of a *k* is typical in Eastern Europe) Schnitzel with Rice.

Sam Skufakiss, a real estate speculator, announced on May 6, 1933, that he and a group he represented said they were investing $10,000 to convert a structure and its surroundings on Calumet Avenue and Standard Street into a real German biergarten. It would, he said, compare with any in the Chicago area. The first floor of the twenty-thousand-square-foot building would have a seating capacity of three hundred with a large dance floor in the middle. The second floor would feature not only a large banquet room but also an indoor space for European-style gardens where families could bring their own food. The building was to open in less than a month. It was quite an undertaking, but what happened, we don't know. It was never mentioned again.

In 1936, the Boulevard Rathskeller was hiring.

Bill Schillo's Antler Cafe and Tap Room. *Calumet Regional Archives, Indiana University Northwest.*

Gruener's Picnic Grove and Beer Garden, "The Coolest Place in Town for Picnics and Parties," was large enough to host large company functions. In 1935, it advertised a big party for members of the Damen and Maenner Choir, an active German music group, who were invited to bring their families. It first is mentioned in newspaper stories in 1909 and seems to have been open until the 1960s.

Bill Schillo of the Antler Inn (and yes, that was the décor—plenty of antlers) on Calumet Avenue in Hammond specialized in German home cooking and Germanic spirits, including chicken, steak and oysters and fish on Fridays. It also offered turkey and chicken dinners for $1.25 per person.

CHOP SUEY, PEKING DUCK
AND OTHER CHINESE FARE

Chop suey, which roughly translates as "bits and pieces," was introduced by Chinese immigrants who came to San Francisco and the West Coast during the gold rush era in the late 1840s and also to work on laying tracks for the transcontinental railroads. At first, chop suey joints most likely fed other immigrants, but chop suey really caught on. It was usually cheap and tasty—what was not to like? In the early 1900s, there was a nationwide chop suey craze across the nation, including in Northwest Indiana.

In 1907, Kong Hong Ho was located at 91 State Street, just a few doors down from King Hung Lo (and yes, it does sound somewhat salacious) in Hammond. A 1913 ad advertised King Hung Low—a slightly different spelling, but the address for both was the same.

That same year, George Lee was the proprietor of the rather fancy-sounding Orpheum Café Chop Suey Restaurant in Hammond.

The Chop Suey Café and Restaurant at 233 East State Street in Hammond opened in 1910.

When you have a craving for chop suey, the time of day shouldn't matter. You need it now! At least that's how it seems looking at old advertisements. In 1910, Yen King Lim Chop Suey and Restaurant was still serving chop suey dinners for twenty-five cents at 2:00 a.m. The Majestic Café, also in Hammond, stayed opened every night until midnight serving such specialties as Blue Points (oysters), Little Neck Clams, Shell Crabs, Lobsters, chili con carne, Chili de Mac, Clam Chowder, Italian Spaghetti, American Chop Suey "and anything you wish to order."

In 1918, the Royal Restaurant in Valparaiso served chop suey day and night. That same year, the New Chop Suey Restaurant opened just a block from King Hung Lo and Kong Hong Ho, advertising "New Place for Good Eats." It also served steaks, fish and oysters, but it was the chop suey that was available at all hours.

In 1921, the Sunday special at Piccolo's Café Lafayette in East Chicago was a roast turkey dinner, but never fear, chop suey lovers, it was available from 11:00 a.m. to 1:00 a.m. The café also offered ravioli, chicken ala king and Lobster Newburg, and in 1921, it boasted that its chop suey and chow mein were made by a first-class Chinese chef.

It may have just been a chop suey joint, but in 1924, owner Sam Chink had standards. Chink, the owner of the New Idea Chop Suey House, was upset when a late-night diner named Gibbons ordered a plate of the dish and then pulled out a flask of whiskey. Sam objected, but the patron insisted he had every right to drink his own booze—which, by the way, was illegal at the time. The police were called, and Gibbons was taken away. "What's the world coming to?" Gibbons wanted to know. After all, this was Chinatown, where he seemed to think laws didn't apply. The story, which originally ran in the *Hammond Times*, became nationwide news, appearing in numerous papers coast to coast, from the *Brooklyn Daily Eagle* in New York to the *Bakersfield Californian*.

In 1927, the American Grill in Hammond advertised that it was famous for its chop suey and southern fried chicken.

The Christmas dinner menu at Bloch's Hotel and Restaurant in Valparaiso on December 22 featured the usual selections one might expect for a holiday meal—roast turkey, chicken or duck; roast leg of lamb; sirloin of beef; and fresh ham. Less expected was the American chop suey with steamed rice. And consider this: the cost of that dish—fifty cents—was only ten cents less than a leg of veal and all the other meat dishes listed above except for the birds. And just to mix it up a little more, the soup served was Chicken Molliganatwy (and yes, that's the way it was spelled, though I'm assuming it's really Mulligatawny, a type of Indian curry soup). Just to mix up the ethnicity of the offerings a little more, the dessert that came with the meal was an English Plum Pudding with Wine Sauce.

It's kind of a rule of thumb: whenever you can't remember what nation you're in, you're most likely in Northwest Indiana. But let's go on with the chop suey.

On May 11, 1929, the restaurant advertised "Chicken Dinners, 65-cents and 75-cents. Chop Suey Dinner, 50-cents. All Day Sunday." In 1934, it

A 1910 postcard shows the newly opened General Electric Hotel located between Fourth and Fifth Avenues and Adams Street in Gary. *Calumet Regional Archives, Indiana University Northwest.*

was selling Chinese Mushroom Chop Suey for 25 cents a pint and 50 cents a quart.

Bloch, by the way, also specialized in fish. In 1929, its fried halibut dinners cost fifty cents. In 1931, it was selling Baltimore oysters by the pint (thirty cents) and quart (sixty cents). It crossed ethnic lines by serving hot tamales for ten cents each and homemade chili. In 1934, it ran a special—a glass of beer and a lake perch sandwich for fifteen cents.

Cam-Lan opened in 1938 in Hammond, the first Chinese restaurant in Northwest Indiana, according to its advertisements. It was an upscale place with starched tablecloths and high-backed booths, and owner Charles Sang always wore a suit. It offered elaborate Chinese dishes, including Peking duck served with its head on (call ahead and ask for the head to be taken off, people advised—the phone number was WE1-511), though the restaurant advertised chop suey as being its specialty. Like most Chinese restaurants in the Midwest, it also offered American food like fried chicken and seafood for those not willing to try the more esoteric chop suey, Genuine Chinese Egg Roll, Cantonese-style fried shrimp and chow mein.

The restaurant also figured in Jean Parker Shepherd's bestselling book *A Christmas Story.* Shepherd, known as Shep, lived briefly in East Chicago after moving from Chicago with his family but spent most of his youth in Hammond, graduating from Hammond High School in 1939. A radio and TV personality, writer and actor, he wrote such books as *In God We Trust, All Others Pay Cash* and Wanda Hickey's *Night of Golden Memories: And Other Disasters.* His humor style was said to be a precursor to that of Garrison Keillor.

Still immensely popular in Northwest Indiana, Shepherd's *A Christmas Story*, based on his days growing up in the Hessville neighborhood of Hammond, was made into a movie in 1983. One of the scenes involves the "smelly hound dogs" that lived in a rundown house next door rushing in and devouring their Christmas turkey. The only place open was a nearby Chinese restaurant, and the closest they could get to turkey was Peking duck, but they decided to call it Chinese turkey, in keeping with the holiday.

Ming-Lang, a Cantonese restaurant, opened in Miller Beach in the mid-1900s and was a downtown mainstay until closing in 2011.

SOCIAL HALLS

It's always intriguing why some ethnic groups open restaurants when they first immigrate to the United States and others don't. Greeks, Asians, Italians and Swedes typically did back then. As far as we know, there was never a Romanian, Serbian or Croatian restaurant in Northwest Indiana. It just seems like the Romanians and other Eastern European immigrants were less likely to open a stuffed cabbage place and instead formed social clubs where the ladies from the community cooked and the men downed shots of slovitz or something similar.

For Romanians, it was Transylvania Hall, a large building located at the corner of Pennsylvania Avenue and Washington Street. The hall opened in the very early 1900s and was torn down in 1972.

For Serbs who migrated to Northwest Indiana after World War II, the Serbian Hall was the place to meet. Both halls were in Indiana Harbor because that's where the largest Romanian and Serbian populations were in Northwest Indiana. But in other towns and cities, there were halls for other ethnic groups such as Greeks, Italians and Croatians, among others.

But Greeks had their halls and churches where Greek food was served at functions, and there were also numerous Greek restaurants throughout Northwest Indiana. I can tell this joke because my aunt Daneise Delahanos— now that's a Greek name—told it to me.

A 1920s photo of the Transylvania Hall in Indiana Harbor. *East Chicago Public Library*.

Transylvania Hall. *Author photo*.

"What happens when two Greeks meet?" she would ask and then answer, "They shake hands and open a restaurant." Then she'd go back to making noodles from scratch, big pans of moussaka and pastitsio and, for dessert, baklava. Even though I'd heard the joke many, many times, I always laughed because I wanted to be invited over again.

In an interesting look at the transmigration or fusion of food cultures, according to Mary Ben-Young, whose parents emigrated from Romania and lived on Pennsylvania Avenue in Indiana Harbor, during the mid-1900s the neighborhood around Transylvania Hall changed. Taco Joe's opened up next door, and a window was cut into the wall separating the two buildings. That way, those visiting the hall could get a taco fix.

OLD COUNTRY PICNICS

Gary had a large Hungarian population or colony, as it was called. It wasn't uncommon to see caravans of cars decorated with flowers and streamers carrying a bride and groom dressed in the wedding finery of their country. Following them would be parents of the couple, members of the wedding party and guests, all heading to the reception, horns honking just in case anyone missed them.

Every ethnic group celebrated weddings in the traditions of their homeland and also held annual picnics in the summer where there was folk dancing, singing and traditional fare to eat and drink. To buy the ingredients needed, there were grocery stores, meat markets and bakeries specializing in traditional foodstuff from each country. Polish meat markets offered a variety of Polish hams and cured meats, and Greek bakeries were the place to go for breads and pastries (pitas, eliopsomos, tiropitas and aptos). The DeRosa family opened an Italian grocery store in Indiana Harbor in the 1920s, and by the 1990s, the store had relocated to Griffith, Indiana, and was being run by the founder's grandson and had started to stock Eastern European foods as well. It was the kind of place where you could choose from an assortment of feta cheeses from different countries. German meat markets often had what looked like one hundred types of sausages hanging above the workspace. A customer would point to the one they wanted, and the butcher would pull it down, hack off the amount requested, wrap it in butcher paper and tie it with a string before handing it to the customer.

AN ITALIAN STORY

There were—and still are—a multitude of Italian restaurants in Northwest Indiana, but this one story stood out, as it was told by a good friend of ours about her mother's brother.

Corrado Bianchino emigrated from Italy, first working as a chef in New York City before coming to Gary, where he owned a restaurant called Ramona's on Fifth Avenue. "He had this special recipe called polenta alla spianatora or polenta on the table," says his granddaughter Angela McCovitz, a personal chef who lives in Miller Beach. "He'd make a real thick polenta and pour it over a wooden table and cover it with rich meat sauce, and people would eat it like that." It's a dish, if you Google it, that can only be found in a few high-end Italian restaurants today, so it's nice to know that Angela's relatives were among the first to serve it in the United States.

And by the way, her take on owning an Italian restaurant in Gary back in the 1920s and over the next few decades was that you had to be in the mob or at least know someone who was so they'd take care of your place by firebombing the nearby competition.

Hey, what are friends for?

Sorrento Inn in Highland was locally known for its great Italian American dinners. *Steven R. Shook Collection.*

HOOCH—HOMEMADE AND OTHERWISE

When Peter Stankowitz, who ran a taxi line, was arrested for using his taxis to deliver bootlegged booze, one wry policeman picked up a bottle labeled "bourbon" and took a sniff. "Say," he said, "if a glass of this was set on a steel plate it would burn a hole through it."

Northwest Indiana was that kind of place where bootlegged alcohol was so common that the police made jokes about confiscated booze. Indiana Harbor had the highest number of bootlegging offenses, with East Chicago second in line, according to the *Times* in a headline story that ran on November 5, 1918. It seems that of fifty indictments handed down in Lake County, all but one were from Indiana Harbor and East Chicago. Now does that mean that there was no booze being consumed in other towns and cities, or does it mean they just had better protection from judges and police? Just asking.

And by the way, while researching this book, I happened upon a newspaper article from the 1920s. It turns out my Romanian grandfather Jon Simon, who owned a dairy, liked other drinks besides milk. He was busted for making homemade wine during Prohibition. He paid a small fine (it was always a wink and a nod in Indiana Harbor), and I'm sure went back to bottling more of his vino.

One of several saloons owned by the Meyer family, circa 1910. *East Chicago Public Library.*

Indeed, Mary Ben Young, whose family lived on the second floor of my grandparents' dairy, told me that open railroad cars loaded with grapes made their way from Southwest Michigan, where they were grown, into Indiana Harbor. Eastern Europeans (like my grandfather, I'm guessing) were waiting to buy bushels of Concords to take home. I'm sure just to eat, right?

Chapter 6

Drive-Ins, Taverns, Gambling Joints and Just Like Ma's

Later, Edward Bartholomew Antonio Sarti couldn't remember if it was Bobby or Jack who stopped by Sarti's Restaurant and Lounge in East Chicago. Both Kennedy brothers were visiting spots throughout Lake County when Jack was campaigning for the presidency in 1960. Heck, their mom, Rose Kennedy, even made a stop at the Red Lantern, that swank beach joint in the dunes.

On January 15, 1934, John Dillinger wasn't at Sarti's campaigning; he was getting ready to rob the beautiful Neoclassical First National Bank of East Chicago just a few miles straight west on Chicago Avenue. After a few shots, he and his accomplices headed to the bank, their clothes somewhat bulky because of the bulletproof vests. Dillinger carried a valise. Inside was a machine gun, which he pulled out and started shooting when the police blocked their exit. The robbers pocketed $20,000 and left Policeman Patrick O'Malley dying on the sidewalk. O'Malley's wife fainted when she heard the news and had to be placed under a doctor's care. He also left three young daughters behind. As an aside, Region historian Arch McKinlay notes in his book *Twin City: A Pictorial History of East Chicago* that "had their research been more thorough, they might have done even better. Not knowing about an elevator that led down to another vault, they left behind a half million dollars."

Dillinger was arrested and locked up in the Crown Point Jail. He managed to escape but not before posing for a photo. According to McKinlay, "Just prior to Dillinger's escaping from Crown Point jail, allegedly with a gun

The Auditorium, built by Cecil Cohen and then operated by his daughter Anna Cohen Fishman, had a saloon and restaurant, and boxing matches were held upstairs. *East Chicago Public Library.*

whittled from wood, a photo taken by Reed Thomson gained wide circulation throughout the state and nation. It showed prosecuting attorney and would-be governor Robert Estill of Indiana Harbor with his arm around the desperado."

East Chicago would get Dillinger in the end. He was betrayed by Ana Cumpănaș, better known to history as Anna Sage, a brothel keeper in Indiana Harbor. Faced with deportation, she made a deal with the FBI to avoid being sent back to Romania. Sage set Dillinger up, and the police shot him dead in front of the Biograph Theatre in Chicago. But things ultimately didn't go well for Anna. She was deported to Timișoara, Romania, two years after Dillinger's death. She died there in 1947 of liver disease.

Dillinger's last ride—to the Crown Hill Cemetery in Indianapolis, where he was buried—made a stop. While his coffin sat in the back of the hearse, the drivers stopped for lunch at Nu-Joy's in Kentland. Then he left Northwest Indiana for good.

The Sartis—Italian immigrants—were a restaurant family. In the early 1920s, Amelia and Andrew, the parents of Denny, Eddie and Reno, opened a soda fountain at 139th and Main Streets in Indiana Harbor, where they also sold plates of their special spaghetti sauce for twenty-five cents.

In 1938, Andrew Sarti and Sam Benedetto opened Sam and Henry's on Chicago Avenue. At the time, fifteen cents got you a shot of whiskey; if you wanted the best stuff, it cost twenty cents more.

Reno Sarti bought his parents out in 1962, and the name changed to Sam and Reno. Ed had just graduated from East Chicago Washington that year and soon after started working at the bar. In 1970, after buying out Benedetto, Reno and Ed changed the name to Sarti's Restaurant and Lounge.

It was the kind of bar that catered to the factory workers coming off their shifts and merchant marines—the Port of Indiana Harbor was one of the largest on Lake Michigan. Before he murdered eight nursing students on the South Side of Chicago, one of the Merchant Marines liked to drink at Sarti's. After the awful news hit the papers, the FBI stopped by to check to see if Richard Speck had come back around.

When Reno died, his kids Scott Sarti and Sandy Roach inherited the business. Scott told a newspaper reporter about the rough clientele his uncle and father had to deal with. The bar did a great business and was often jampacked at 3:00 p.m. when the first shift at the mill ended. Second shift ending also filled the bar, and the end of the midnight shift brought just as many thirsty guys. But that many men drinking too much booze often meant problems, and the brothers sometimes got a little bloody interfering in fights.

Ed Sarti retired after forty-five years, and the bar was sold. It was certainly a long run.

WOMEN NOT WANTED

A woman's place was in the home and not in a tavern or bar back in the 1800s and early 1900s (and in some states even later). A tavern was a place for men to get away from nagging women and screaming kids after a hard day of work.

In early times, it was so segregated that when stagecoaches pulled to a stop at an inn, the men headed to the bar section, where there might even be a sign stating that no women were allowed, to chew tobacco, smoke cigars and drink. Women were relegated to another room with their children. You know, those tired, hungry and cranky kids who had just been confined in a stagecoach bumping up and down on horrible roads for the last eight or ten or more hours. I wonder what those women thought as their husbands' laughter could be heard from the next room as they imbibed.

But before the temperance movement started in the mid-1800s, there was a lot of drinking by everyone. It sounds like an excuse, but water really wasn't safe to drink. Thus, it wasn't unusual to start imbibing in the morning and sip throughout the day. In 1790, Americans consumed an average of 5.8 gallons of pure alcohol a year, as they typically started their day with a dram or about 1.5 fluid ounces of whiskey, rum or applejack. At lunch, there was another slug or two, ale with supper followed by a nightcap before bed. And we're not just talking about men. Women and children drank, and even toddlers might be given the sweet dregs from the fermented peach juice and apple cider that was made in rural areas (and a lot of America was country back then). By 1830, about the time Northwest Indiana was being settled and stagecoaches started making their way along the Sauk Trail, consumption had risen to 7.1 gallons a year.

All this gave rise to the beginnings of temperance leagues and ultimately, though it was a long way off, Prohibition.

PROTECTING WOMEN FROM
THE EVILS OF ALCOHOL

The state of Michigan once had a law on the books forbidding women from working as bartenders in all cities with a population of fifty thousand or more unless they were the wife or daughter of the male owner. The United States Supreme Court upheld that law in the case of *Goesaert v. Cleary* in 1948. Yes, 1948.

"We cannot give ear to the suggestion that the real impulse behind this legislation was an unchivalrous desire of male bartenders to try to monopolize the calling," said Justice Felix Frankfurter, who was usually considered a progressive. Not in this case, though. Women, the court believed, needed to be protected from their own vulnerabilities when it came to alcohol.

When there was no stopping women—say because there was no other place for them to eat when the stagecoach pulled to a stop—they often had their own side door for entrances and exits.

There were risks with women though. Sometimes wives would come in, crying or yelling because their husbands were drinking away the rent and food money, the kids were hungry or needed medical care and they were scared because the landlord had just threatened to evict the family, putting them and all their possessions out on the street. You know, like we said, nagging women upsetting a man's time for relaxation.

Out in rural areas like the Brass Tavern, a stagecoach stop owned by Allen and Julia Watkins Brass, running the place was a joint effort. Julia put up food, made wine, cooked and served the meals, did the washing up and tended the kitchen garden at the Brass Tavern. No one complained, as far as we know, about her doing all that work. But then again, it was the country and in the middle of nowhere.

In a post–Civil War photo taken of the Svets family, Swedish immigrants who owned a great deal of farmland in what is now Munster, they are seen in a photo standing on the porch of their tavern. Though the tavern isn't much to look at, everyone—men, women and children—most likely pitched in to keep the place going. As Munster didn't become a city until 1907, gender issues regarding bartending were moot for a long time.

Even further back, from 1836 to 1844, Miss Holmes, the maiden sister of Edgar Holmes, who owned a farm in Portage Township, opened a tavern near the farm along with Edgar's wife's maiden sister, Miss Rugar. It became known as the Old Maid's Tavern. One traveler didn't know what to expect, but when he stopped, he was met by refined and cultured pioneer maidens accompanied by their two very large Mastiff dogs. Their tavern and inn,

Duffy's Castle was located on Ridge Road in Munster in the '60s through the '70s. *Kenneth Schoon.*

located near Willow Creek, was described as the neatest, with the best food and most comfortable lodging anywhere nearby. The double log cabin, stable and corral were built in part by the two "old maids," who helped cut trees and build the cabin. Edgar Holmes died, and his wife and the women continued operating the inn, adding more structures to accommodate more guests as they could, including a whole four-horse stagecoach load of passengers. Being one of the few stagecoach stops at the time, it was at times overcrowded. James H. Luther, who drove a freight wagon between Chicago and LaPorte for several years, remembered sleeping with four dozen others in the bunks or, at times, in the feed yard.

There was excitement during the years it was open. Francis Staves, who was accused of killing John Pelton, was discovered there wiping blood off his saddle, and it was where James Adams stopped to rest for the first time on his wild horseback ride to round up soldiers from Fort Dearborn (Chicago) to Detroit, which was under an imminent attack by Native Americans. It was a marathon ride, accomplished in twenty-eight hours, with Adams changing horses every fourteen to fifteen hours.

"I made the trip in 28 hours and seven minutes, getting to Fort Dearborn at 8 p.m. on January 3, 1837," he said. Harriet Martineau, the British writer who visited the United States, visited the tavern as well.

Solon Robinson, who owned an inn in Valparaiso, predicted that "those women will all be married soon, 'cause there's several men hereabouts looking for the Holmes." And so it came to pass. The owners married, and the Old Maid's Tavern closed.

YOU CAN STILL DRINK THE WHISKEY

The Hub, a saloon and cigar kind of place in Miller Beach, featured I.W. Harper whiskey, a Kentucky whiskey whose roots go back to 1848, when I.W. Harper immigrated to this country with just four dollars in his pockets. Twenty-two years later, he founded Bernheim Bros. Distillery, and in 1872, they began making I.W. Harper, an award-winning whiskey that won gold medals into the early 1900s. It was also advertised on a sign outside the Amazon Restaurant. The company is still making I.W. Harper bourbon, but both restaurants are long gone.

THE JOHNS

John Henry Tinsley, the first African American in East Chicago, opened Hamburger John's, where burgers sold for a nickel.

John seemed a popular name for dining establishments throughout The Region. In East Chicago alone, there was John's Bar on Alder, which advertised that it served beer, wine, liquor and, almost as an afterthought, lunch. If you wanted to order in advance, just tell the operator to call IH 3327 because back then there were no dials. John Sarantis opened John's Eat Shop in the early 1920s and sold it to a young Greek man in 1975, indicating that he ran the business for half a century. John Collins opened Hot Dog John's on Exchange Street in East Chicago in the 1920s. He owned it, along with his wife, Mary, for about forty years. The restaurant went through several other owners until closing after almost seventy years in business.

Mike Dosen, who manages the Facebook page "East Chicago, Indiana in Photos," points out that John's Eat Shop was on Main Street in Indiana Harbor and Hot Dog John's was on Exchange Avenue in East Chicago. The latter was known as HDJ. "HDJ was always the go to place after a night out," says Wally Jakubin. "In the late 1950s they sold them eight for $1.00 all wrapped in that blue, yellow, and red dotted bread paper," says Jimmy Calinski.

I guess we know what John's Chili Dogs sold.

But in case you're not confused, let's add one more. There was a John's Hot Dogs on Columbus Avenue in Indiana Harbor. In an interesting aside, Hot Dog John's was next door to the 825 Club, one of the well-established gambling joints in the city, and that's a story we'll discuss in a bit.

John Klobuchar co-owned Little John's Tavern in East Chicago in the 1960s and '70s.

John and I's Rib Den and Lounge in Hammond featured, you guessed it, barbecue ribs, though it also had New York strip steak specials on the weekend for $6.95. Meals came with a relish tray (does anyone do that anymore?), salad and choice of potato.

Then there was John and Shirley's and John's Never Inn, which advertised "Sellin' Sociability," had great softball teams from the late 1940s to the 1960s and at times played against, in what must have caused some confusion, John's Bar, also in East Chicago.

John's Billiards in Gary was owned by John Anton. You could grab a pie at John's Pizzeria in Griffith or dine at the more upscale-sounding Jonathan's in Highland.

WHAT'S IN A NAME

Their names might not have been John, but using either first or last names was a way of connecting to would-be customers—or that's the conclusion given all the bars, restaurants and taverns named after their owners.

In 1956, a list of licensed pinball operators included numerous examples.

In Whiting, Edward Matsuko and Paul Vladika owned Ed & Paul's Sportsmen's Club.

In East Gary, there was Edward Sherman's Bar and Grill and Tony Vaccaro's Tony's Corner, and Pete's Tavern and Bud's Tavern were in Cedar Lake.

Frank's Tap, Andy's Tavern, Ted and Charley's Tavern and Denny's (owned by Denny Nichols) were all in Gary.

East Chicago had a bunch: Frank's Inn, Chuck and Irene's Bar at 719 West 151st Street in East Chicago, Marko's Tavern, Milan Skrtic owned Milan's Place, Fred Saviano owned Saviano's Tavern and Emil Bernal owned Emil's, at 5048 Reading. We can see why Matt Domakowski used his first name for Matt's Bar. There was an Eddie's Bar but no last name associated with it.

In Chesterton, you could dine at Bob's Grill.

There were pinball machines at Jack's Tap in East Chicago, but we don't know of any at Jack's Restaurant in Munster. Same goes for Wally's Café, a nice-looking place one-half mile from Dyer.

WALLY'S CAFE

ON ROUTE 30 — ½ MILE WEST OF DYER, IND.

Opposite: Wally's Cafe, located one-half mile from Dyer, opened in 1939. *Steven R. Shook Collection.*

Above: Jack's Restaurant, circa 1950s, on the northwest corner of Calumet Avenue at Ridge Road in Munster. *Steven R. Shook Collection.*

THERE'S A DAME BEHIND THE BAR

Surprisingly, there were also a lot of places owned by women, some with their names and others more discreet.

In Cedar Lake, Genevieve Fetta owned the Silver Dollar Inn, Emma Ross owned the Cedar Inn and Mabel Gross had Downing's Café.

Lorraine Major owned the Lighthouse Tavern in Hebron, but she was very busy. With her husband, Erwalt (known as Shorty), she also managed the Gary Boat Club around the same time and took over management of the Fran-Dene Inn on U.S. 30, two miles east of Highway 53 or one mile west of Ainsworth Road. The Friday specials were lake perch, both bone-in and boneless, and shrimp. There was also May's Delicatessen in Hammond.

Edna Wilks owned a restaurant named, interestingly, Tasterite Restaurant in Chesterton.

In Dyer, Elizabeth Sharkozy had Sharkey's Tavern; Alma's Café, owned by Alma Downer; Mary Ashcraft's Coffee Pot; and Jo Ann's Restaurant, owned by Anna Sum.

In Gary, Rodmilla Jackovich ran the Workingman's Tavern, Martha Chrison owned Liberty Lunch, Eva Baker had her B&O Lunch, Adank's Tavern was owned by Lucille Adank, there was Betty's Bar at 502 148th Street, Rose Kocher's R&K Lunch and Ruby Moore had Charley's Tavern. Velma Melton had Uptown Lunch on Broadway, Dorothy Meinborg had the Sandwich Shop and Emma Evancho was the owner of George's Bar.

East Chicago had several women-owned places, such Ann Stiglitz's Stiglitz Bar at 501 Emlyn Place, Beatrice De Beneditto's Bea and Rock's and Doris Dohlin's the Old Corner Tap on Chicago Avenue. Carmen Christiana owned Carmen's Pizza.

DANCING THE NIGHT AWAY

Floor shows seemed to be big in 1935. Lithe drawings of women in tropical bikinis flanked the advertisements for dining roast pig on rye and dancing at Popeye's New and Enlarged Beer Garden in Hammond. Al's Tavern, also in Hammond, had another drawing of a woman in a bikini, but this one had on large angel wings and high heels. A couple months later, there were no angel wings or even a bikini—she was naked. The big floor show there was headed by Carroll Abbott doing comedy, dance and songs. Skippy Carmon (maybe she was the one with angel wings) danced the rhumba and snake hips. The master of ceremony was Jack (Bozo) Mason; there was no cover charge, and dinner options were fish, chicken, steak, oysters and frog legs. The drawing of the woman with angel wings appears again for Neil's Barn Yard in Gary, which despite its name, advertised that it was "Lake County's Finest Night Club" with complete floor shows each night. There were no drawings of scantily clothed women in the ad for Whitey's Dine and Dance in Hammond—just lake perch, no cover charge, good parking and good music.

DEW DROP INN

As far as we know, none of the Dew Drop Inns were owned by men named John, but one, with a slightly different spelling, was owned by a woman. Starting in the 1930s up until the 1990s, there were either three bars with that name or they moved to new locations frequently. There was a Dew Drop Inn on Guthrie in Indiana Harbor, another on Burr Street in Gary and one (or maybe two) on Sheffield and also Cline in Hammond.

And then there was Margaret Buckmaster, who owned the Du Drop Inn at 3838 Main Street in East Chicago.

When it comes to interesting names, we have to give kudos to the Black Cat in Ainsworth, now part of Hobart. It was a restaurant and café open all year round.

JUST LIKE MA WOULD HAVE MADE IF ONLY SHE KNEW HOW TO COOK

When it came to home-style cooking, in 1938, Ernie Gu opened Ernie's Fireside Inn on Heaton Street in Kouts, a local favorite famous for such specialties as perch sandwich, prime rib, chicken livers and a foot of onion rings. A photo of the restaurant taken in 1950 shows signs in the window advertising Minit Steak Sandwiches for fifteen cents and the daily availability of freshly churned buttermilk. Inside, you could enjoy your Minit Steak and glass of buttermilk while listening to jukebox tunes. Twenty-two years later, Ernie retired and closed his little eatery.

Corrado Bianchino emigrated from Italy, first working as a chef in New York City before coming to Gary, where he owned a restaurant called Ramona's on Fifth Avenue in the 1930s. The Old Style Inn in Valparaiso opened in 1932 and did an eighty-five-year run before closing in 2017. An old-fashioned sort of place with dark wood paneling, it was totally Region-centric when it came to its menu—steaks, all-you-can-eat frog legs, lake perch, blue gill, duck, pasta, walleye and crab legs, along with its signature menu item: prime rib served every day. You could get baked squash if you didn't want potatoes, and on St. Patrick's Day, there was always corned beef and cabbage. This being The Region, on Friday and Saturday nights, there were crisp and tender frog legs for $2.75, as well as oysters for $2.50. If the price seems high, remember the salad bar was included.

Hilliard's in Kouts advertised "Food You're Sure to Enjoy," offering a choice of twelve entrées served every Sunday, plus a special every Saturday of chicken and homemade noodles, Swiss steak or broiled ham for one dollar. Wednesday's fried chicken special also cost one dollar.

Marie's, with its sophisticated pastel-colored interior and Sky Room where one could sip a cocktail, most likely light a cigarette and listen to the

Marie's Sky-Line Motel and Steak House was the epitome of the sleek and low-slung, with lots of glass and linear lines known as mid-century modern that was popular in the 1950s and 1960s. *Steven R. Shook Collection.*

piano playing, advertised a special Thanksgiving Day menu. The place was known for its steaks, fried chicken and pie and was open every day from 7:00 a.m. to 11:00 p.m.

Lovey's on East Lincolnway sold its charbroiled steak sandwiches for fifty cents—not a bad deal at all.

Sauzer's Little Waffle Shop at the crossroads of U.S. 41 and U.S. 30 in Dyer specialized in waffles and hot cakes, though it also advertised serving a variety of sandwiches and light lunches. Next door was Sauzer's Kiddieland Amusement Park that opened in 1950. There were rides for both young and old kids, including a miniature train, carousel, two sizes of Ferris wheels, bumper cars and a Tilt-A-Wheel. Those who had Bowman milk delivered to their house could save the paper lids on the glass bottles and trade them in for discounts at the amusement park.

"East Chicago, among its rich history, was also known for its social places," says Terri Thomas. "It was said there was a bar on every corner. I remember Fred's Tap, corner of Indianapolis and 151st Street, a place to have a few drinks and their fish fries on Fridays. My favorite place for fish, however, was Puntillos on Indianapolis Boulevard. Their shrimp and fish were fantastic."

A bonus for those eating at Sauzer's Little Waffle Shop on the busy intersection of U.S. 31 and U.S. 41. in Schererville was the fifteen-acre Sauzer's Kiddieland right next door. *Steven R. Shook Collection.*

Sauzer's Little Waffle Shop, open twenty-four hours a day, was famous for its waffles. It also served steaks, chicken and fish and was known for its home-style cooked luncheons. *Steven R. Shook Collection.*

Photographer Guy Rhodes looked up a 1915 Sanborn fire insurance map of East Chicago on the Library of Congress website. Posting a photo of the 500 block of West 143rd, he highlighted no fewer than five buildings on the block labeled "Sal" (saloon). "It was clear what the afterhours prerogative of the industry workers was then," he writes.

Margie Trevino suggested going way back to the Sandbar on 135th and Deodar, owned by a judge and his wife. She said it had a restaurant in the back of the bar that served the best fish. "His wife and her sister ran the kitchen," she said.

Emil's at 151st and Reading in East Chicago had such specials as chicken livers and mushrooms for one dollar and Emil's Harvest-Style Chicken Dinners for the family.

The Cotton Lounge at 151st and Railroad Avenue in East Chicago advertised fish dinners for eighty-five cents, steaks, frog legs, chicken, shrimp and pierogi—a Polish dish that's still so popular in Northwest Indiana today that Whiting holds an annual Pierogi Fest that attracts 250,000 people a year and was named one year by *Oprah* magazine as one of the top ten festivals in the United States.

Tivoli's, on Tod Avenue in East Chicago, also had frog legs, as well as lake perch, steaks and shrimp. It advertised rock-and-roll music as well, from 9:30 p.m. to 1:00 a.m.

Don Hill, who grew up in East Chicago, remembers Joe's Tap and the Riviera Restaurant that was in back. "You had to walk a narrow sidewalk to the rear entrance to the dining room," says Hill. "My aunt worked as a waitress there in the evenings as a second job. The food was awesome, with authentic Italian pasta sauce made from scratch and simmered for hours. To this day, I've never tasted a sauce that comes even close. And their steaks—brought to your table on sizzling platters. This goes back to the mid-1960s."

OLD-TIME DINER

The Trolley Diner, an old railroad car fashioned into a restaurant located on Guthrie Street near the entrance to Inland Steel in Indiana Harbor, opened way back in the 1930s, before converting train cars into restaurants became retro cool. It was the kind of place where you could take home a whole bag of hamburgers for fifteen cents, which was five cents more than a burger at

White Castle. It also served such "just like ma would have made" dishes as meatloaf, roast beef, mashed potatoes (real spuds) and gravy and homemade pies baked fresh daily. In the 1930s, the softball team the Trolley Diner Hot Dogs were serious players, participating in the Hammond Amateur Softball Association against such teams as the Bill Meisel–Chester Tavern and the Florence Tavern. Got to love the names.

In the 1950s and '60s, the diner was owned by a guy nicknamed Duchie, and besides the great food, people often would drive around the back of the place to see Caesar and Nardi, two great Danes, and Tubby, a small Collie. Jimmy Calinski, who ate there for twenty-five years, remembers taking the dogs for a run in the once vast prairie (later turned into subdivisions called, appropriately, Prairie Park) near Franklin Elementary School. "Best food ever," he recalled.

While the Saturday special at Cataldi's Brothers in Hammond was stuffed beef tenderloin with homemade Italian sauce, the restaurant also had chicken, steak, chops and other Italian specialties.

THAT'S SO REGION

In 2013, after seventy years in business and a name change, the New Country Lounge in Hobart closed its doors. This was due in part, according to the owners, to the Indiana state laws that banned indoor smoking. Formerly known as the Country Lounge before its last name change in 2011, it was considered a "Hobart institution."

Indiana University Northwest professor emeritus James Lane, a historian who writes the popular "Northwest Indiana Historian James Lane Blog," used to take his classes there at the end of the semester. He recalled that its nickname was Hunky Hollow, as it was frequented by Eastern European politicians, and for those wanting to be in the know and make connections, it was the place. "In fact, caricatures of old-time regulars lined the walls," Lane writes on a blog post.

Lane pointed out how the derogatory term "Hunky," originally used disparagingly to describe Slavic immigrants, became a badge of pride for some white ethnic Region politicians. In fact, it was so much about Region politics that, according to Lane, "when Danilo Orescanin became IUN chancellor in 1975, President John Ryan recommended he hang out at Country Lounge to socialize with area muckety-mucks. Orescanin would

The San Remo in Griffith. *Author photo.*

scribble names and phone numbers on a placemat and ask his secretary to type his hen scratching's."

File that under "That's So Region," a way of taking derogatory epithets about the area and turning them into positives. Long looked down on by other parts of the state because of its heavy industrialization, large amounts of immigrants and ethnic composition, Northwest Indiana has reframed such sayings as "Region Rats" and the use of words misspoken by those learning the language such as "deese" for these, "dose" for those and "da" as in "Da Region" as a tribute—based on being tough, adaptable and cool.

As for Region Rats, Joseph S. Pete, an award-winning journalist who works for the *Times of Northwest Indiana*, writes about what was meant as a pejorative. "It's derogatory for downstaters who view the region as a polluted, gang-infested urban wasteland that's overrun by indicted politicians. But it's a badge of honor. One blogger said you're a Region Rat if you know roads are just a place for trains to park, school isn't canceled unless there is at least 20 feet of snow and you drink pop, not soda."

NOT JUST FOR THANKSGIVING ANYMORE

What started as a turkey farm owned by Dr. Walter and Bess Thrun in the early 1930s became a Northwest Indiana classic for seventy-five years, not closing until 2015. Deciding not only to raise turkeys but also serve them to travelers passing by on U.S. 30, Bess opened the twenty-eight-seat Strongbow Turkey Inn just across the highway from the turkey farm in 1938. Processing the turkeys they raised, the Thruns became famous for their turkey pies, smoked turkeys and whole turkey dinners, as well as steaks and sandwiches. They also started a successful mail-order business, shipping turkeys, both fresh and smoked, through the United States.

Though turkeys ruled—murals of the birds graced the walls—there were other distinctive features, such as the aviation-themed bar linked to a landing strip at the nearby county airport. But most stunning of all were the five hundred or so rosebushes Bess tended, all in a variety of colors and types.

When Walter died in 1951, his daughter Caroline Thrun Adams and her husband, Chuck, took over, and by the end of the decade, they had modernized the kitchen and expanded the restaurant to accommodate some 250 diners. By 1993, when their son Russ and his wife, Nancy Adams, bought the restaurant, a banquet facility capable of serving around 500 patrons had been added. The staff numbered 130. The space and capacity were needed, as the restaurant served 250,000 turkey dinners a year.

Chicago Tribune columnist Phil Potempa dined there often growing up and was good friends with Russ Adams, Bess's grandson, who was the executive chef at the time. Potempa says he felt like King Henry VIII (we're trusting Phil hasn't indulged in one of the king's other hobbies—that of cutting off the heads of unwanted wives) "feasting on their decadent turkey liver pate with diced onions and crackers for my starter course, and then, herald the arrival of flavorful dark meat from an enormous turkey leg dinner served with mashed potatoes and sage dressing, all smothered in gravy, for my main event."

A cookbook author as well, Potempa said that among the many recipe requests from Strongbow's that he gets are their sumptuous turkey schnitzel and scrumptious "Bess's Turkey Salad Bowl."

It was the kind of place that attracted celebrities. Orville Redenbacher, the popcorn magnate who hailed from Valparaiso, would dine there when he visited his hometown. Potempa also noted that other notables who dined there include *Wagon Train* TV actor Robert Horton, acclaimed culinary hero and kitchen personality Chef Louis Szathmary, radio icon Paul Harvey,

Specializing in all things turkey, the Strongbow Inn started off as a turkey farm whose owners took it to the next level and sold meals at a roadside diner. *Steven R. Shook Collection.*

children's doctor and TV personality Dr. Lendon Smith, country music legend Conway Twitty, U.S. Supreme Court justice Sandra Day O'Connor and nearly every Indiana governor elected since 1940. Colonel Sanders of Kentucky Fried Chicken fame didn't object to a turkey dinner. A friend of the Thruns, he stopped in when visiting The Region to check on his restaurants.

Russ Adams shared his favorite celebrity story with Phil, recalling a time when he was working in the kitchen and Los Angeles Dodgers manager Tommy Lasorda walked through the swinging doors connecting to the dining room. He'd ordered a turkey sandwich and told Adams to load it up, adding, "And make it like you're making it for your brother."

Spike's Lakeside Inn 2 was originally located on the East Side of Chicago before moving to Schererville, where it was known for its seafood offerings including perch, coconut shrimp and whitefish, as well as frog legs, chicken parmesan, barbecue baby back ribs and pork chops. Each meal was accompanied with an all-you-could-eat salad bar filled with containers of leaf lettuce, coleslaw, kidney bean salad, peaches, broccoli and cheddar salad, pudding and so much more. Now that it's Greg's Place, many of the same menu items remain, with new additions as well.

We don't know much about Kay and Danny's Greenhouse, located in the Roxanna district of East Chicago, but the name is intriguing.

CARHOPS AND DRIVE-INS

The 1960s marked the beginning of the end of the drive-in's reign, supplanted by the even more quick and convenient fast-food places where you grabbed your food to go. But back in the day, such places as the Lure, which had locations in Portage and Gary, were the place to go for burgers, hot ham and cheese and roast beef sandwiches, fries, shakes and the supersized "Big Lure."

Carhops dressed in cute little uniforms brought the food to your car at Ted's Drive-In near U.S. 20 and U.S. 12 in Miller Beach.

Merriman's, a steak and chops sort of place in Highland that offered "modern air conditioning" as well as complete fountain service, started offering drive-in services in the early 1950s so "you can enjoy our delicious chicken, shrimp, or fish in a basket in your car."

Hannon's Drive-in, located on the northwest corner of Washington Street at U.S. 30 in Valparaiso, was easy to recognize because of its huge sign in the shape of a frosted mug of root beer. Menu items included burgers, corn dogs, onion rings, fries, Hannon's root beer made on site and the Big John, named after owner John Hannon. That was a hot dog served on grilled white bread served by carhops. It sounds good, but unfortunately, Hannon's closed in 1998.

In 1956, Max and Bob's Merriman Drive In in Highland offered a baker's dozen of hamburgers—order twelve and get thirteen. The burgers cost twenty-two cents each, hot dogs were eighteen cents and Coca-Cola and root beer went for eight cents. *Author photo.*

Anyone who traveled U.S. 12 and U.S. 20 in Miller Beach back in the 1960s and 1970s most likely recalls the twenty-foot Frankenstein's monster statue in front of the Frank 'n Stein Drive-In. Holding a foamy mug of root beer and a hot dog, it may have been too close to the A&W Root Beer nearby. But who wouldn't love the concept and the play on words. The statue stayed up for a while after the place shut down, but alas, that is gone now too.

A MAIN STREET STALWART

Doña Carmen Valenzuela opened El Patio on Main Street in East Chicago in the 1960s. It was a small Mexican restaurant, but that doesn't mean they didn't jazz it up. The entire dining area (there was a separate room with a counter where people, mostly men, gathered to chat and drink coffee) was entirely covered in elaborate mosaics—a job that must have taken hundreds of hours. The menu offerings were tacos (both hard and soft), sopes, tamales, burritos, tostados, menudo (beef tripe soup), chile rellenos, fish soup, shrimp dumplings, flautas and, surprisingly, pork chops and liver and onions. It was open from early morning (people on their way to Inland Steel would stop beforehand for breakfast, and there were such dishes as chile con carne with scrambled eggs, rice and beans) until late at night.

You could peer into the pass-through window into the kitchen and see the large stoves with big pots of pork stewing in red adobo sauce and refried beans, the mashing of fresh avocados for guacamole and the piles of just-grated cotija cheese. The waitresses were friendly and efficient, calling their female customers *chica* and children *cariño*. They didn't speak much English, but all you had to do was say the names of the dishes you wanted to eat, and they would soon appear in the pass-through and be brought steaming to the table. The price of a meal included refried beans, salad, rice and a big basket of flour tortillas. Homemade hot sauces, in a range of spiciness, already sat on the table.

After thirty-seven years of managing her restaurant and doing the cooking, Valenzuela sold the restaurant, and it had several owners. The last was Esmerelda Germain, who purchased El Patio in 1998, running it until she had to close the doors in 2006 because of a redevelopment project,

Here's the background. For decades, since El Patio opened in the 1960s, Main Street flourished, but slowly, stores and businesses—particularly in the one-block area where El Patio was located—either closed or moved their businesses to other cities in Northwest Indiana. El Patio finally was the only business open on the street, and it still attracted customers despite the rather bombed-out aspect of the block. It finally closed, not because of lack of business but because the city decided to tear everything down for a redevelopment project. Still, almost fifty years wasn't bad. The only sad thing was where did all the retired millworkers, the ones who sat at the counter and drank coffee and told their stories in Spanish, go once it closed?

ROLL THE DIE AND KEEP AN EYE OUT
FOR THE COPPERS

In 1892, Roby, a small community on the Illinois-Indiana state line, was the destination for a horse racing track and boxing arena able to accommodate twelve thousand spectators. With its success, two more tracks were established, these on Indianapolis Boulevard near where many of the successful fish shacks such as Phil and Vogel's were located. At the time, all was legal, but that didn't last long. Laws were passed, but they didn't end gambling in Northwest Indiana, not by a long shot. It just called for more ingenuity. According to Hal Lay, who writes the blog "A Short History of Gambling in East Chicago," in 1901, Johnny "Fix-'Em" Condon established the Long Beach Turf Exchange, a gambling joint featuring a special amenity—a special train to transport gamblers from Chicago—that would be frequently used in the future.

Johnny sent out invitations that read:

> *You are invited to the finest equipped and only Monte Carlo in America, delightfully situated in Lake County, Ind., near the Standard Oil Company's Works at Whiting. No "interference" from county or State officials. Open the year around....Ample accommodations for 5000 people....Why go to the racetracks when you can come here and play all the races at... Washington Park, Brighton Beach, Fort Erie, Newport, St. Louis, Harlem and Hawthorne....All the finest brands of wines, liquors and cigars.*

Lay also shares a quote from journalist Herbert Asbury, who described the turf club as "the most extraordinary gambling house ever projected in the United States—a castle protected by stockades, barbed wire and picket fences, armed lookouts in sentry boxes, alarm boxes, ferocious bloodhounds…and

The Roby Cafe in the Whiting/Hammond area. *Steven R. Shook Collection.*

with tunnels leading outside the grounds and arrangements for setting fire to the place if the police succeeded in gaining an entrance."

Johnny had planned the place to be a resort on the water with all sorts of buildings for gambling, drinking, dining and betting. But there was a problem—too much publicity. Within months of opening, the state shut it down.

Enter James Patrick "Jim" O'Leary, the son of Patrick and Catherine O'Leary whose cow was said to have kicked over the lantern that torched their barn and then the entire city during the Great Chicago Fire in 1871. Jim was only two at the time. The family lost basically everything in the fire, and in the neighborhood where Jim lived, he learned a lot of basics on how to survive. His early employment consisted of working for bookies and then becoming a bookie himself. He was known for keeping his word and paying his debts, and his gambling business thrived. It was said he'd take bets on anything.

But in that kind of business, you're always one step ahead of the law, and in 1904, he transferred some of his business to the *City of Traverse*, a steamship that left the docks from Illinois Central in South Chicago with one thousand players aboard. Sometimes they headed to Northwest Indiana, staying out until the day's racing winners had been announced. It was a pretty complicated set-up. An autorun tube transmission sent from the roof of a railroad building gave the odds and results to those on board. In 1907, without the type of mob protection to keep going, the *City of Traverse* was dry docked. Gambling, however, went on.

O'Leary also revitalized, for a time, the Long Beach Turf Exchange, which reopened for the winter. It was so popular that the Lake Shore Railroad put on four suburban trains to carry patrons between the Exchange and Chicago.

Here's the story of Hal Layer, professor emeritus, San Francisco State University. A graduate of Roosevelt High School in East Chicago, Layer is the grandson of Harold Layer, also known as Tiger, who was as colorful a character as could be. He spent his career working at the Big House, a longtime and well-known gambling joint located at 3326 Michigan Avenue in Indiana Harbor. Indeed, the place was so infamous that when U.S. senator Estes Kefauver's Special Senate Committee to Investigate Organized Crime set its sights on interstate commerce in 1950, part of his focus was on the Big House.

"The Big House, a gambling place operated by William Gardner, Sonny Sheetz, and Harry Hyades, who have close connections with the Chicago syndicate, took in $9,000,000 in 1948," writes Region historian Archibald McKinlay. A columnist for the *Times of Northwest Indiana* and author of several books on The Region's history, including *Twin City: A Pictorial History of East Chicago, Indiana* and *Chicago's Neighboring South Shore: Lake County, Indiana*, McKinlay described the Big House as "Chicagoland's casino of casinos, thanks to the early backing of Frank Nitti." Nitti, who was one of Al Capone's top henchmen, had the rather daunting nickname of "The Enforcer." If you were running a gambling enterprise, you'd certainly want to be on his good side.

Sure, there was a lot of smoke from cigars and cigarettes, sloshing of whiskey and other drinks and women looking to make money off the men who were winning, but it wasn't totally a dive. Indeed, according to Layer's website, the Big House was reported to maintain "a free taxi service to and from Chicago's south side.…One of the Midwest's most lavish gambling emporiums…[it was also] the racing wire nerve center of all bookie establishments in the county. It boasted Oriental rugs on the floor of the second story, which housed costly mahogany roulette and dice tables.…Roughly 125 persons were employed in the place.…The Big House also had 15 branch handbooks, six in Hammond, two in Whiting and seven in East Chicago."

The Chicago Crime Commission also started investigating, and though the Big House closed, it didn't really slow down the immediate relaying of racing results to Hammond, East Chicago or Whiting. That's because, according to Layer, the wire service continued from a hideout in Cedar Lake.

The heat was on, and Sonny Sheetz and Peck Gardner decided to take a powder, ignoring their indictments issued by a Lake County Grand Jury. The investigation also corralled several East Chicago officials, including Mayor Frank Migas, because they weren't enforcing gambling laws. But then again, if you have people backed by Frank Nitti offering you money to look the other way, would you really want to say no?

There were other issues as well. Peck and Sonny had somehow forgotten to pay $1,054,430 in taxes on $2,348,271 in gambling profits—it happens, you know. They agreed to pay $750,000 to avoid trial. Luckily for them, the hard-charging prosecutor who was after them lost his job in the next election, and Metro Holovachka, the new prosecutor, dismissed the charges. Holovachka had his issues with the law and would later be disbarred for taking bribes. Interestingly, Peck had been a successful athlete and student in Indiana Harbor, a war hero and then a policeman—that's where he met and befriended mobsters. That's how things worked in East Chicago. And everyone knew it.

But where there's a market, there are people to supply what the market demands. And thus the 825 Club, also known as the South Shore Smoker, became one of the gambling venues that stepped forward to supply the action. It was located at 825 West Chicago Avenue, hence its name, and was in business from 1949 to the 1970s.

It was a top-notch organization, at least according to one reporter who said that upon entering, he found himself in one of the biggest and best-equipped gambling joints he'd ever seen. "It was a long room, brilliantly lighted with overhead lights, and there must have been 40 or 50 men milling around listening to race results coming in over a loudspeaker." Other reporters surmised that the Big House and 825 Club were the forerunners to Las Vegas.

The 825 Club—like other similar places such as Forsythe Recreation and Billiards Club, also in East Chicago, and Four Acres Recreation Club in Roby by the Illinois-Indiana state line, as well as others in the Calumet region—continued running without much interference from local authorities. Indeed, they often received advance information when a raid was scheduled to be conducted. The most popular time for a raid was before elections.

Layer pointed out that East Chicago was one of the very few cities with passenger train tracks and service in a central downtown location from 1906 to 1956. This provided easy access to gambling in East Chicago for customers from Chicago, Hammond, Gary, Michigan City and South Bend.

A STORIED BUT CHECKERED PAST

Pete and Mabel's Tavern on the corner of Michigan and Parrish Avenue in East Chicago was a longtime favorite for customers and a big headache for law enforcement. Owned by Pete and Mabel Harretos, it was known as a place to drink, eat and, if you were a man on your own, buy some company.

Wondering why it was so quiet on the night he stopped by on June 19, 1967, a reporter for the *Hammond Times* was told by a waitress that "the Feds were in town." And indeed, the place, one among several, was busted for being what the paper described euphemistically as a "B-Den." Ironically, they also noted that while women bartended, waitressed and befriended men, it was still illegal in Indiana for them to sit at the bar to drink.

The tavern, which opened for business in the 1950s, was run by the couple until Pete's death in 1991. Mabel continued on after that, assisted by her three sons. She died in 2006, leaving behind those three sons, nine grandchildren and thirteen great-grandchildren. Though it had its shady side, it was an East Chicago institution for decades.

Chapter 7

Fish Joints and Perch Palaces

When settlers first arrived, Whiting, located on Lake Michigan, was mostly swampland broken up only by ridges of sand dunes that ran parallel to Lake Michigan. There were at least five inland lakes, including the three that remain—Wolf, Calumet and George—as well as Hyde and Berry, which the late Archibald McKinlay, a longtime chronicler of the Calumet region, recalled as being "Eden-like, full of fish and water lilies, its banks lush with berries, especially raspberries, and luxuriant with woods, topped at the lake's northern end by birches that stood like sentinels guarding a magic place."

Like at the inland lakes in Cedar Lake and Porter County, hunting and fishing lodges were established in the late 1800s, attracting sportsmen from all over. It was a beautiful area, and local lore has it that Abraham and Mary Lincoln came here often with their children to swim when they were in Chicago.

This wilderness changed, first with the advent of the railroad in 1851 and then with Lever Brothers producing 450 pounds of soap in the 1880s and the opening of Standard Oil not long after. The bucolic scenery might be gradually disappearing, but the proximity to Chicago brought customers from the city to visit fish joints that sprung up to catch, cook and serve freshly caught fish. Old-time restaurateurs like the Vogels actually pastured their cattle in the prairies surrounding the Lever Brothers plant. That's so typical Region—nature and urban.

Because the region abounded with frogs, their legs were, just like the plentiful perch, sautéed in butter until tender and golden brown.

Al Knapp's Restaurant and Lounge, Roby. *Steven R. Shook Collection.*

Whiting became the nexus for fish joints. Many came and went quickly, such as Smith and Bader's around 1894, the Little Restaurant in 1896, the Lake Shore Buffet and the White House, which burned down in 1910. Even the restaurants that would become enormous, capable of seating between five hundred and one thousand people, started off as places that could hold ten to twelve.

But though most of these started off as joints, with perch scooped up from the lake, boned and pan fried and sold for cheap, many morphed into high-end restaurants with large banquet facilities and seating capable of handling one thousand diners at a time. Judging by how Margaret's Geneva House advertised real floors, many must have had floors made of packed dirt or sand.

VOGEL'S

One of ten children born in 1890, Fred Vogel quit school in fifth grade after his father's early death at age thirty-six so he could help his family financially. In a move we can barely imagine today, Vogel took over his dad's

Vogel's Restaurant started off as a fish joint and became a much more sophisticated dining experience. *Author photo.*

job distributing barrels of beer for the Fox Head Brewing Company. The beer was delivered from Milwaukee, Wisconsin, by train and stored in a building at 117th and Cleveland Avenue in Whiting, Indiana. From there, Vogel loaded it up and transported it by horse and carriage to Hammond. But he wasn't the only one working. His mother and two of his sisters ran a grocery store.

At one of his beer stops, Vogel met Ida Lauer, who had emigrated from Erfelt, Germany, in 1909 at age seventeen. Ida didn't speak English, but Fred spoke German, having learned it from his mother. Happiness to have someone to speak to turned into love, and the two married in 1910. By 1913, they had two children, and in 1915, they opened a boardinghouse and saloon. Ida must have run it at least during the day because Fred was also working at the Whiting refinery. But his plan was to go beyond a saloon; he wanted both to be his own boss and also to own a larger restaurant. At the time, Whiting was a nexus for high-end dining places, including Phil Smidt's, Pete Levent's, George Levent's, Dave Lungren's, Margaret's Geneva House, Hammond Beach Inn, Roby Inn and Camp Cunio. His plans were interrupted when he served overseas during World War I.

We know all this because Jan Vogel Hahn, the daughter of Bob Vogel and the granddaughter of Fred and Ida, wrote her family history about thirty years ago when Vogel's was one of *the* places to dine. It is available on the Whiting-Robertsdale Historical Society's website.

Other fish specialty places included Lundgren's and Levent's, which was established in 1924. Their postcard read, "Located at 1247 Calumet Avenue, Whiting Indiana. 14 Miles South of Chicago's Loop. One-half Block North of U.S. Routes 12, 20, & 41. Specializing in chicken, steak, frog legs, and seafood dinners. We cater to banquets and parties in any of our seven dining rooms. Open the year 'round. Fully air-conditioned."

"A building was available at 2501 Calumet near Sheffield Avenue," writes Hahn. "It was located on the road that cuts across Lake George and enters Calumet College. Fred spent different hours of the day for weeks watching the traffic, tallying license plates, and realized it would be a good location for a restaurant."

Closing their boardinghouse in 1921, Fred and Ida opened Vogel's, which could seat 100 customers. A fire destroyed the building, but the couple rebuilt, and within a few years, because business was so good, they added on to accommodate 350 more diners.

Whiting is right on Lake Michigan, and one of the favorites served at Vogel's was boned and buttered perch. "In the early 1930's frog legs became another specialty dinner item," writes Hahn, noting that both of Fred and Ida's sons, Bill and Bob, started a frog farm behind the restaurant on Lake George. But demand was so high that they couldn't raise enough frogs, so they started getting them from southern states, including Florida. By the 1990s, the majority of frogs were imported from Bangladesh.

A change in traffic patterns and other issues forced the Vogels to relocate, and in 1944, they opened a new restaurant on Indianapolis Boulevard large enough to seat one thousand people.

Ida and Fred's sons were running the business, but Bill wanted to go out on his own. He opened a drive-in restaurant and then later the Flame in Gary, another upscale restaurant. He passed away in 1963.

Business boomed for quite some time, but then the Skyway and Indiana Toll Road were built, bypassing Whiting for those traveling to and from Chicago. Then came the casinos. At first, many assumed that the casinos would bring more business to the area and would be good for all, restaurants included. But casinos turned out to be a closed-door system, so to speak. To encourage their customers to stay on the premises (and to keep them gambling), they had their own restaurants with cheap drinks and food. And then came another blow to business. "The regulations put on perch fishing for commercial fishermen has forced us to raise our prices and has given us another hurdle to jump over," Hahn wrote. "It has become almost impossible for us to get fresh perch."

Other restaurants in Whiting also felt the pain. It was a death knell, though some held on longer than others. We'll get to that later.

Sadly, after three-quarters of a century in business, Vogel's closed on September 28, 1997.

PRINCE OF PERCH

Probably the most iconic of Whiting's restaurants, one with a national reputation, was Phil Smidt's.

A reporter wrote decades ago:

> *The story of how Phil Smidt's began is quite charming. California bound were Phil Smidt and his new wife Marie in 1910. When the train stopped in Roby for water, the Smidts got off the train thinking they were already in Chicago where they would switch trains. Well, the train left without them and there they were, in Roby. Making the best of the situation, the Smidts, like many other entrepreneurs in the increasingly popular recreation area around Five Points at the turn of the century, opened a restaurant. With a $600 loan, they opened the first Phil Smidt's fish house. There was seating for twelve, a bar and boat livery. Smidt's was one of many fish houses to be found there.*

Marie, it turns out, was quite a cook and could pan fry perch to perfection. The restaurant had an all-you-can-eat policy, and for forty cents, customers were served perch, vegetables and rye bread. A stein of Utah Brau, the house beer, was, of course, extra. Despite its name, Utah Brau, a mix of Utah barley and Bohemian hops tagged as "America's Finest Beer" and "America's Famous Beer," was made by Standard Brewing Company in nearby Chicago. When Prohibition shut Standard down, mobsters, including Capone's gang, took over its manufacturing equipment until they got in trouble for tax evasion and the property was seized by the government.

Phil and Marie's son Pete and his wife, Irene, were running the business in the late 1920s. Things didn't slow down even during the Great Depression.

I mean, we're talking about Whiting, Indiana, yet Phil Smidt's had its share of celebrities stop by for dinner, including Babe Ruth, Jack Dempsey, Gene Tunney, Mayor Richard J. Daley, Bob Hope, Betsy Palmer (though

Phil Smidt's. *Steven R. Shook Collection.*

she grew up next door in East Chicago, Indiana) and the Prince of Wales. Jimmy Cagney showed up for a bond rally that Pete held to raise money for the war effort.

In an interview, a former Whiting resident named Wayne Stiller recalled when Phil Smidt's was first located at the Wolf River Bridge where it crossed Indianapolis Avenue, the major road connecting Chicago to Indiana. Wayne was four when his family moved next door to another classic, Lundgren's Fish House on Calumet Avenue.

"Phil Smidt and Sons set a standard by which few in the restaurant business can be compared," recalled Robert Mecklin, who started dining at the restaurant when he was young. "I remember my father (who was an executive at Amoco Oil) taking my family to Smidt's for dinner, and the orders we placed were boned and buttered perch, frog legs and, of course, the ever-popular side dishes of cottage cheese, beets, potato salad and dessert was the famous pies and cakes."

Disaster struck in 1945 when an underground gas pipe exploded, killing two patrons, injuring nineteen and demolishing the restaurant. "I was delivering newspapers there the day it blew up. I was about eleven or twelve at the time," wrote Wayne Stiller, who noted that Pete, an avid hunter, kept ammunition in the basement. "I could hear what bystanders said was ammunition blowing up in the fire."

Whatever caused the explosion, Phil Smidt's moved into what had been the original Lundgren's Restaurant on Calumet Avenue and Railroad Street not far from where one of the casinos would be built. In 1980, Mike Probst, who had worked for the restaurant for four years and had a degree in restaurant management from the Sulzberger Hotelfachschule in Bad Hofgastein, Austria, purchased the place with his brother. Two decades later, they sold it to David and Barbara Welch, who sadly became the last owners.

After ninety-seven years, Phil Smidt's shut its doors for the last time on October 20, 2007.

MARGARET'S GENEVA HOUSE

Edward and Sophia Winkelried opened the Geneva House in 1913 in Five Points, just south of the Hammond Bathing Beach in a section of the city known as Robertsdale (though their location was also given as Whiting in some articles and advertisement). Edward Winkelried, whose parents were also in the restaurant business, was born in Geneva, Switzerland (hence the name), and Sophia emigrated from Germany. Their restaurant was known for its European style of elegance, including white tablecloths and professional-level service. Oddly, or maybe it was a sign of the kind of flooring found in some of the other fish places, it was noted for its "real floors." Besides that, they advertised steam heat and being open year-round.

When Edward died in 1926, a newspaper headline identified him as "proprietor of the Geneva House, one of the best known of the Robertsdale fish houses." Like its counterparts at Vogel, Lundgren's and Smidt's, the Geneva House was known for its pan-fried perch, frog legs, hand-cut steaks and fried chicken. Another restaurant, Al Knapp's, had not only perch and frog legs on its menu but also rainbow trout from the Rocky Mountains, Florida red snapper, live Maine lobsters (a one-pound lobster was $5.75), scallops, walleye pike and genuine turtle soup. The latter cost $0.50.

After her husband's death, Sophia ran the restaurant for another decade or so, and when she retired, their daughter Margaret Winkelried Carroll took over, changing the name to Margaret's Geneva House. Besides running the front of the house, one source says she did most of the cooking herself. Much of her clientele came from Chicago, but locals from nearby cities like East Chicago also dined there frequently. Margaret's Geneva House was in business for over eighty years.

Edward and Sophia Winkelried emigrated from Switzerland and Germany, respectively, and opened the Geneva House, named after Edward's hometown, in 1913. *Whiting-Robertsdale Historic Society.*

The sixty-six-room Illiana Hotel stood at the southeast corner of 119th Street and Atchison Avenue in Whiting. *Commonwealth.*

It's intriguing that these places with similar menus—even down to the assortment of sides such as coleslaw, cottage cheese, potato salad, pickled beets and kidney bean salad, along with an assortment of breads including rye that were delivered to the table with every order—were so similar yet so different. They could handle huge banquets, wedding receptions and other events.

According to the Whiting-Robertsdale Historical Society, for its grand opening on March 19, 1928, the Illiana Hotel served such fare as broiled tenderloin steak, spring vegetable soup, buttered California asparagus, young celery hearts, Idaho potatoes and a deep-sea shrimp salad. For dessert, there was a special layer cake and ice cream. We don't know what the Illiana's Special Coffee was, but it was on the menu along with cigars and mints.

THE EVOLUTION OF A RESTAURANT: LEVENT'S TO DIAMOND'S CHARCOAL-BROILED STEAKS

First Charles Levent's (Peter Levent's restaurant), established in 1924, was located at 1247 Calumet Avenue in Whiting, but they obviously knew their market was across the state line and advertised that they were just fourteen miles south of Chicago's Loop and one-half block north of U.S. Routes 12, 20 and 41. They advertised that they specialized in chicken, steak, frog legs and seafood dinners; catered to banquets and parties in any of the seven dining rooms; and were open year-round. And they were fully air conditioned.

The building later became Juster's Charcoal Broiled Steaks and then after that George Diamond's. Another steak house, Diamond also owned five other restaurants, including one in Chicago and another in Las Vegas. It was the kind of place where the steaks were grilled over an open flame. One of their house-made salad dressings was so unique that even now, you find people searching for the recipe online. It was a Russian dressing, but more pink than red, and it appears, if what's online is true, that it was made with cans of tomato soup. I had it, I loved it and I still remember it.

Diamond was a famous Chicago restaurateur with a place on Wabash in the city said to be all done up in 1950s swank—all red velvet and red upholstery—and to have cost $1 million to remodel. Besides the restaurants he owned, he was planning on opening another venue in Acapulco, Mexico.

A popular Whiting steak house, Juster's later became George Diamond's. *Author photo.*

THE LYNDORA

In November 1935, Amelia Earhart dined on turkey served at the Lyndora Hotel in Hammond. She wore a blue printed dinner frock with a white jacket and was described as being "this lithe feminine person."

The local couple who sat next to her asked what aviators ate in flight. "We're only beginning to know something about the diet problem for fliers," she told them. "We know partially how to feed a football team but we're just starting on what aviators should eat. I know a couple of dieticians whom I've tried to interest in this."

Tomato juice was her choice of liquid when flying, she said. But as the evening at the Lyndora was coming to a close and many of the diners were jittery from downing too much coffee, Earhart was drinking a glass of buttermilk.

The Lyndora Hotel was the sort of place where you might run into someone like Amelia. Situated at the corner of Calumet Avenue and Highland Street, even its coffee shop was handsomely and expensively decorated.

Those attending the Musical Dinner Program on August 27, 1922, enjoyed such vocal performances as "Sweet Indiana Home" and "By the Sapphire Sea" while a violinist played "Liebe Freund" and Schubert's "Serenade."

Lyndora Hotel, (Owned by Standard Steel Car Co.) Hammond, Ind. 3-hir

For many years, the Lyndora Hotel was considered the best in Hammond. *Steven R. Shook Collection.*

The one-dollar dinner, served from 12:30 to 2:30 p.m., offered the following choices: Potage Ala Reine, Consommé Julienne, Hearts of Celery, Queen Olives, Boiled Ox Tongue, Piquant Sauce, Braised Veal Sweetbreads with Mushrooms, Roast Spring Chicken stuffed and served with Giblet Sauce, Roast Loin of Pork, Fresh Apple Sauces, Potatoes Ala Cream, June Peas, Combination Salad and either Fresh Peach Shortcake or Ice Cream and Cake.

In case you're wondering, Potage à la Reine is a rich cream soup made with chicken and almonds, though when the aristocratic Tudor family ate it in the 1500s, partridge was used instead of chicken. Consommé Julienne, a classic French soup made with chicken stock and vegetables that are finely shredded, also has an ancient pedigree.

"It's the leading social club of Lake County," said A.C. Werner, the manager of the Lyndora Hotel in 1925. He added that each evening, people from the surrounding cities could be found dining here. "Heads of industries, judges, the most brilliant members of the bar, physicians, educators, clergymen, big businessmen and other successful men in Lake County come to the Lyndora to dine," he said.

In 1938, the stately Lyndora had new owners: the Mercy Sisters of St. Vincent, who bought the largest hotel in Hammond with plans to run it as a commercial hostelry as well as a place for the aged.

WITH A VIEW OF INLAND STEEL

Excursion boats and yachts plied the waters past the newly built steel mills to dock at the South Bay Hotel, a large stone edifice with a wide front porch overlooking the vast blue expanse of beach and Lake Michigan. And then, with a tilt of the head, there were the chimneys belching smoke from the blast furnaces of the sprawling Inland Steel mills. It didn't matter. Yachtsmen from Chicago came to dine, play cards, dance and enjoy gaiety well into the night. The hotel was built by Owen F. Aldis, described as a wealthy, erudite Vermont lawyer, who had moved to Chicago to practice real estate law for East Coast investors. The hotel, known as the "Atlantic City of the West," was managed for years by the attractive Bertha K. Chittenden, described as a widow of wealth and refinement who seemed to know how to please the mostly male guests but also ran a tight ship and managed to make the hotel profitable. The hotel was all elegance, with gourmet food, porcelain tubs in every room (yes, back then that was worth advertising in the *Chicago Tribune*) and other refinements necessary to please rich, idle men as well as executives in town to do business at the mill. Chittenden had a three-year contract to run the hotel and built up a moneyed clientele. Seeing how successful she was, the management tried to wrest control from her early, but a court case found in her favor.

The South Bay Hotel was a grand place in Indiana Harbor just down the beach from Inland Steel to the north. *Author photo.*

We don't know much about Bertha. She was born Bertha Kadish in Chicago in 1856, the daughter of Theodore Kadish and Emma Freund, who appeared to have emigrated from the Czech Republic or Austria. On February 12, 1879, at the age of twenty-three, Bertha married Daniel Shaw, who was twelve years her senior. In 1900, she was managing the Hyde Park Hotel in the upper-class Hyde Park section of Chicago under the name of Chittenden and listed as a widow. We don't know what happened to Mr. Shaw or who Mr. Chittenden was. We do know that, sadly, she had a son named George Shaw who played football for Purdue University and was one of several students who died in a train wreck on their way to Indianapolis for a big game in 1903. He was seventeen years old. His mother's name is listed as Bertha Kadish.

As far as the hotel, when Kadish/Shaw/Chittenden was managing the place in 1900, it was described as one of the first generations of "French flats," so called apartment buildings built for permanent residents but that had the typical arrangement of spaces such as lobbies and the specialized services offered by hotels. Shortly after that, she would move to Indiana Harbor to take over the South Bay Hotel. In 1910, she would again be living in Chicago with her daughter Olivia Shaw.

HISTORIC MARKTOWN

The sidewalks and landscaping now complete, the Mark Hotel had one of the best restaurants in all of East Chicago. The second-floor ballroom was used for banquets and corporate parties throughout the year. Located in Marktown, a planned community for employees of Clayton Mark's steel pipe manufacturing firm, the hotel was designed by famed Chicago architect Howard Van Doren Shaw in the English Tudor Revival style in 1917. Now in the National Register of Historic Places, all except for three of the original two hundred residential homes were built with stucco exteriors. This idea of company housing is also found in the Sunnyside section of Indiana Harbor, planned originally for workers at Inland Steel.

CHEF O'DONNELL AND THE GARY HOTEL

Visitors to Gary were amazed at the culinary excellence found in the dining room at the Gary Hotel, at the time a fourteen-story building that would later be replaced by a ten-story structure. Built and owned by one of the steel companies, it was later leased by a New York hotelier named George O'Donnell, who had worked at the Waldorf. It was said that Judge Gary, for whom the city was named, was so impressed that he called his home in New York to talk about the dinner he'd just been served.

Remember, we're talking Gary, Indiana, here. O'Donnell gave up his leases and opened a saloon later that year, in 1910, connected to a steak and oyster house on Sibley Avenue in Hammond. He ordered the oysters from Baltimore, and they arrived daily on the express car of the fast-moving Baltimore and Ohio train. Before shipping, they were loaded into barrels filled with sea water, and then the barrels were nailed shut and immersed in ice. The oysters' salty tastiness and freshness was such that people came in droves from Chicago to dine at O'Donnell's restaurant.

The restaurateur liked to boast that the oysters taken out of Chesapeake Bay in the morning would be served by his restaurant for dinner the following day.

Representing the city's large German population at the time, the lavish Gary Hotel had a rathskeller in its basement. *Calumet Regional Archives, Indiana University Northwest.*

Oysters, I understand after reading an article about O'Donnell's bivalves in the November 12, 1912 issue of the *Times*, get testy when they're hungry. Or at least that's what it seemed to a local politician by the name of McCracken. He'd heard about the freshness of O'Donnell's oysters and asked the restaurant to send five dozen to his home. O'Donnell complied. Unfortunately, McCracken for some reason concluded that the bivalves were hungry and went to feed the largest of them. Why he didn't just eat them, I don't know. But the oyster's response was to snap its shell on his fingers, resulting in a lot of pain. He spoke to newsmen about the ordeal, his fingers heavily bandaged. "O'Donnell should be compelled to feed these oysters every morning and not let them starve," McCracken grumbled to a news reporter. "If he did they wouldn't be so vicious."

Whether McCracken attempted to introduce a law to make oyster owners feed their bivalves, we don't know. As for oysters, it all came to an end when O'Donnell passed away. One newsman who enjoyed hanging out at his restaurant lamented that there were no longer fresh oysters anywhere in Lake County.

As for the Gary Hotel, after moving into a new building at 647 Broadway in 1911, it was not only a hotel but also the location of the Gary Commercial Club and Chamber of Commerce. Their offices and reception rooms were located on the first floor. The club rooms on the mezzanine floor were considered among the most palatial in the state. The hotel's English Grille also was super posh, with its beamed oak ceiling and quaint carved figures of medieval monks. The Italian Renaissance period was re-created by yards of heavy linen frieze drapes, French tile flooring, Gothic windows, specialty constructed torchieres, accented walnut columns and other flourishes, including Sicilian lamp bases and imported Aubusson tapestries.

The Norton Hotel, which opened on Sixth Avenue near Broadway in Gary in 1908, advertised having all the delicacies of your own table. As for the rooms, an article in the *Times* said they were as fine as any in the city, with each one having cold and hot running water and several fine bathrooms in connection. We take that to mean you had to walk down the hall and share a bathroom with others.

THE BOOMERANG

The menu at the Boomerang Dining Room in the Hotel Lembke located on U.S. 30 in Valparaiso featured roast prime rib of beef, steak, seafood and chops all cooked on their open-hearth broiler. The five-story hotel was built around 1924 at a cost of about $130,000—serious money back then, particularly since Valparaiso was still a relatively small town. But it was a solid place, made of concrete and steel, said to be fireproof. The interior was finished with carved oak and rosewood panels. In 1988, it was torn down to make way for a parking lot.

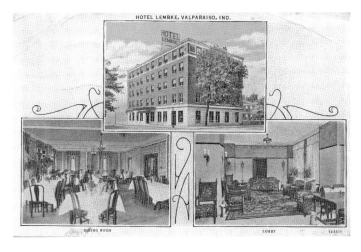

Top: Built in 1923 by Charles Lembke, a noted Valparaiso architect and contractor, Hotel Lembke at 23 North Lafayette on U.S. 30 in Valparaiso, seen here circa 1928, was razed in 1988. *Steven R. Shook Collection.*

Bottom: The Boomerang Dining Room at the Hotel Lembke in downtown Valparaiso featured roast prime rib of beef, steak, chops and seafoods cooked on the open-hearth broiler. *Steven R. Shook Collection.*

FRAN-DENE INN

The Fran-Dene Inn in Hobart was in operation for at least twenty years, from the 1940s to the 1960s. Advertising "Fine Food" stated, "If you're particular about your food, you'll particularly like our cuisine. Every dish expertly prepared to win your compliments."

Cuisine, a common word today, wasn't often used, setting Fran-Dene apart somewhat. In 1942, the restaurant was open for Christmas and featured a full turkey dinner for $2.50. Featured on the menu were steaks, roast beef dinners, chicken, pizza pie (the latter word is almost an archaic term today when we've shortened the dish name to just "pizza"), short orders and sandwiches. The bar was air-conditioned, and specials included barbecue ribs and barbecue chicken on Saturdays, a fish fry on Friday, as well as lake perch (bone-in and boneless) and shrimp and an organ bar (not the entrails but a musical instrument) where musicians such as Jerry Trump played on Friday and Saturday evenings.

As an added benefit, they advertised an air-conditioned bar, beer and wine.

COUNTRY CLUBS AND WOMEN'S CLUBS

Private clubs with fancy clubhouses for members only have been around for a long time, but even women were beginning to get their due—and asking for the right to vote—in the 1890s. Often they were appendages of the men's groups, but it wasn't until the 1920s that women began having clubhouses of their own, though that was still not the norm. There was even a Lake County Federation of Women's Club, an umbrella group.

EQUINE PROBLEMS

In 1952, Chef Dante Mazzari of the Indiana Hotel got in a little trouble by selling beef tenderloin that turned out to be horsemeat. The difference in the price per pound was considerate, as beef was $1.25 per pound and the market price for horse meat was $0.85 per pound.

The 110-acre Woodmar Country Club opened in July 1925 in the Woodmar section of Hammond. The clubhouse, a Tudor Revival building designed by noted architect L. Cosby Bernard, opened on New Year's Eve 1930. *Author photo*.

CLASSIC ITALIAN

Spiccia's in Whiting, owned by Michael and Carmela Spiccia, was known for both its food and hospitality. Mike Spiccia, who first opened his restaurant in 1940, welcomed patrons with open arms, made great pasta dishes and his specialties such as Chicken Vesuvius and also found time to entertain by playing his concertina. After his death in 2001, the restaurant closed.

A BIG CLAIM TO FAME

In 1964, the Jackson Five played for the first time publicly at Mister Lucky's Lounge at 1100 Grant Street in Gary. Recognized by the Rock and Roll Hall of Fame, the family singing group became so popular that they performed there five to seven nights a week. It, too, closed.

FLAMING FOOD

The Patio, located on Broadway in Merrillville, was a restaurant food fans turned to for a fine dining experience, to hold banquets and parties and to hobnob with local politicians. The eatery closed its doors in January 2015 after having been on the Northwest Indiana restaurant scene for more than forty years. It was originally Church's Restaurant and became the Patio under new ownership in 2006. The owners were Greek, loved to cook and developed many of the recipes that were listed on the menu.

The Patio had long been known as a hotspot for politicians to gather, make deals and dine. And it's easy to see why. The Patio was famous for such dishes as veal parmesan, served at both lunch and dinner, and veal picante (thin slices of fresh veal sautéed in Marsala wine with mustard, garlic and slices of lemon). The Greek Steak was tender cuts of beef tenderloin sautéed with mushrooms in wine. Other specialties include Spinach Salad Flambe à la Patio (a spinach salad mix with brandy and salad dressing and then set aflame and served warm). Flaming food was a thing there, as the Steak Diane was also set alight. Other dishes included Shrimp de Jonghe à la Patio, frog legs, lobster tails, stuffed flounder, trout and Alaskan King Crab legs. The side dishes were plentiful: spaghetti or rice pilaf, soup, salad, baked potato or French fries, rolls and either coffee or tea. The average dinner cost nine dollars.

The Cotton Lounge in East Chicago on Railroad Avenue and 151st advertised homemade pierogi, frog legs, chicken, shrimp and steak, as well as fish dinners for seventy-five cents in 1956. The Holiday, also on Railroad Avenue, had a businessman's luncheon for eighty-five cents and a Friday Fish Fry.

HOW SWEET IT WAS

Al Sweet grew up very poor. After his parents divorced, he and his dad moved to Gary, where his dad took a job in the mills. Sweet opened Al's Hamburgers in Hobart before he served overseas during World War II. Upon returning, he teamed up with Leonard Blair, and the two bought the Palm Grove in late 1945. At the time, according to his daughter Candee Sweet, the business was pretty much a strip club before her father took it over. Blair and Sweet moved to a renovated Howard Johnson's on Industrial Highway.

Big Wheel Restaurant on Lincolnway in Valparaiso, shown here seven years after it opened in 1963. *Steven R. Shook Collection.*

Sweet was soon to get another partner as well when a young woman named Connie, hearing that they needed a musician, applied for a job. She was a southern girl, a gifted musician with perfect pitch. But she was a pianist, not an organist, and so couldn't play a Hammond organ, and that's what Al Sweet had. Give her two weeks and she'd learn, she promised. And so she did. The two later married. Connie continued to play, helped manage the restaurants and even learned to do comedy routines with her husband. Their two kids, George and Candee, grew up working in the restaurants.

Sweet opened other restaurants as well. There were the YMCA and YWCA cafeterias—all in Gary—followed by San Remo Restaurant and Lounge at 112 East Ridge Road in Griffith and the Wagon Wheel restaurant in Merrillville, which opened in the '60s.

Formerly the Sorrento Inn, when restaurateur Al Sweet and his business partner Blair bought the business, they changed the name to San Remo. It was a swank place with high-end food.

"We'd serve 1,200 people on a Friday night," said Sweet's daughter, Candee. "That's when we had all-you-could-eat lobster tails and crab. People would wait in line for two hours."

In 1958, the San Remo boasted another unique feature so common for Al Sweet's restaurants: the Festa Cart, a custom-made "artistic and functional craton design." The Festa Cart, which was described in advertising literature as an "epicurean trademark" of San Remo, featured a sumptuous selection of hot gourmet foods. The salad bar displayed dozens of tempting salads and appetizers. There was live music in both the main dining room and lounge.

Sweet described her father as an innovative entrepreneur, saying that the Palm Grove Restaurant had the distinction of being the first air-conditioned dining spot in Lake County.

"When he ran San Remo's, Dad accepted the first credit card used in a restaurant in Indiana, and he also installed the first microwave oven," said Sweet.

Candee said her father opened his first eatery just before World War II in Hobart. It was called Al's Hamburgers. The expansion of Mr. Sweet's businesses continued through the '50s, when he opened a number of popular spots

"Dad totally loved the business he was in and enjoyed promoting what he did best—running a restaurant," Candee Sweet recalled.

HELPING OTHERS

"My dad had a big heart. He spent every Saturday morning at Boys Town and also helped out Trade Winds, an organization for people with disabilities," said Candee Sweet. "There was a fountain at San Remo, and all the money that would go in it, he'd give the money to Trade Winds. He was so happy to be alive. To him, he had won the lottery."

And he always gave back. "I ran into a guy who said to me, 'You're Al Sweet's daughter, aren't you?' and when I said yes, he said, 'Your dad saved my turkey farm,'" recalled Sweet. "The guy was really struggling. The weather had been bad, and he thought he was going to lose everything. My dad told him if he kept those turkeys alive, he'd be there to buy as soon as he could get there."

When Leonard died, all the Sweets, including the kids, had to pitch in to keep the restaurants going. "My dad put crates on the floor so we could reach the sink," said Sweet. "We started peeling carrots and eggs, then we graduated to dishwashing."

There was the super swank Palm Grove located in the oddest place. Originally a fixture on Fifth Avenue near Clark in downtown Gary, the

The menu cover for the Palm Grove Restaurant. *Andrew Prieboy.*

restaurant relocated to Industrial Highway. Its location as part of a strip of land contradicted the sleek glass and brick restaurant, its lights spilling out into the parking lot, that was instantly identifiable by the flashing neon palm tree. But the surroundings beyond the lights were a backdrop of darkened buildings and shadowy lots where old trucks and other large vehicles sat empty and the nearby buildings appeared abandoned, whether they were or not.

In all, the Palm Grove was a rather glamorous place—sleek tables and counters, a softly lit dining room and bar area and pink banquettes. It is isolated among a long line of serious businesses. But it didn't matter to the clientele. It was the kind of place that now, over a half century later, conjures up visions of women in sheath dresses, their shoulders swathed in white or brown mink stoles, sitting in the pink banquettes or at tables covered with crisply starched white tablecloths. There were large ashtrays on those tables and cigarette smoke rising in the air, and the menu called for such decisions as whether to order Shrimp de Jonghe, steaks or go for the once popular throughout the nation but now long-forgotten dish called Chicken-in-the-Rough.

For such a glamorous place, Chicken-in-the-Rough was oddly out of sync but certainly rode the crest of a popular food trend. This dish required a chicken roaster on display turning out one of the restaurant's most popular dishes. The trademarked name with its special cooking methods and proprietary seasoning blend superseded Kentucky Fried Chicken, which wasn't franchised until 1952. Its origins stretched back to 1936, when a down-and-out Depression-era couple named Beverly and Rubye Osborne, their life savings gone, were on the road from their home in Oklahoma to California. When their old pickup truck hit a bump, causing the fried chicken they were carrying in a basket to spill over the floor, Rubye, as she picked up the pieces, made a life-changing statement when she said, "This is really chicken-in-the-rough."

Inspiration hit, and Beverly turned the truck around. They were heading back home and starting a new business—Chicken-in-the-Rough, a business where franchisees used a special griddle that Osbourne developed for frying chicken that was dusted with a proprietary blend of spices. Rubye had to sell her wedding ring to get startup funds so they could open a restaurant. The ultimate dinner was fried chicken with shoestring potatoes and a hot biscuit typically served with honey.

Nowadays, people eat about 20 percent of their meals in cars, but back when the Osbournes first introduced Chicken-in-the-Rough, that concept was much more unique. Cars didn't even have cup holders. Those didn't come about until 1983, when Chrysler added built-in cup holders to its minivans. In the 1920s, Model T cup holder attachments could be ordered after-market from the Sears catalogue. You could get, for your car, kitchenettes, flowerpots and snack trays to add to your vehicle. In 1957, Cadillac offered a pull-out bar with magnetized cups in the glove compartment of its Eldorado Brougham. But for some reason, none of these really caught on—though we're thinking the flowerpot certainly sounds interesting—until the age of minivans.

In 1953, at least two Region restaurants were offering Chicken-in the-Rough. The Palm Grove advertised a Chicken-in-the-Rough special—$0.99 Monday through Thursday, $0.51 less than the weekend price of $1.50. The ad featured a copyrighted drawing of two chickens wearing golf attire looking concerned because their balls had landed in the rough. A newspaper advertisement for the La Salle Grill in Hammond boasted it was the home of Chicken-in-the-Rough.

Around the same time, *Time* magazine ran an article about the business. It turns out chicken had been good to the Osbournes, and they were grossing

The menu at the Palm Grove. *Andrew Prieboy.*

almost $2 million per year, had sold 335 million orders of Chicken-in-the-Rough and had created 250 franchised outlets, including some as far as Johannesburg, South Africa. The Osbournes not only knew how to make some really good chicken, but Beverly also had a lot of marketing savvy, understanding the importance of rousing and maintaining customer interest and recall through the use of logos and trademarks.

But for whatever reason, Chicken-in-the Rough didn't continue to boom. Now, there are fewer than a half dozen places that still license the brand, including Palms Krystal Bar and Grill in Port Huron, Michigan, which opened in 1936. Compared to the Palm Grove prices of 1953, they charge twenty-two dollars for two Chicken-in-the-Rough four-piece dinners. The other places are in Sarnia, Ontario, and Holyoke, Minnesota, and now Oklahoma is supposedly seeing a comeback in places serving this delicacy.

Chapter 8

Still Serving After All These Years

There are doors no longer open to us, rooms where we'll never sit again and meals that we can never savor except through memories.

Oh, to ride again in my parents' big Buick into the pool of light shining from a neon palm tree, briefly casting pink and green shadows over the interior of the car as we stop for dinner at the Palm Grove. To celebrate or mourn family events in one of the elegant rooms at Phil Smidt's in Whiting, watching as waitresses (that's what they called servers back then) carry out trays filled with platters of pan-fried perch, fried chicken and frog legs, or order four tacos dorados (corn tortillas fried and then folded in half and filled with chunks of pork in an adobo sauce) at El Patio on Main Street in Indiana Harbor.

These are gone, one by one, having served the last meal and poured the last shot, said goodbye to the regulars before turning off the lights and locking the doors one final time.

Several studies estimate that up to 90 percent of independent restaurants close during their first year, and the ones surviving those first twelve months have an average five-year life span. Of those still open after their fifth anniversary (and remember we're talking about 90 percent of 10 percent), 90 percent will likely remain in business for a minimum of ten years.

But how long afterward? It varies. Tastes change. Highways redirect traffic in other directions, families sell and the new owners can't carry on for whatever reason in ways that customers want. Inflation, recession, depression and now a pandemic keep diners away.

Teibel's has been a Region classic for almost one hundred years. *Steven R. Shook Collection.*

The oldest restaurant in continuous operation in Indiana is the Log Inn in Haubstadt, in southeast Indiana. When Abraham Lincoln dined there in 1844, this stagecoach inn had already been in business for almost twenty years. That part of the state was settled much earlier than Northwest Indiana, but the Franklin Tavern, formerly the Franklin Hotel, opened in 1857 in a building that was just three years old at the time. It was a railroad hotel, as the tracks ran right in front of the place, and it still is a great place to go for food and drink.

In 1894, John Flannery was granted a tavern license in Chesterton despite the protests of the anti-saloon types. Two years later, when a fire destroyed three buildings on the north side of town, including John and Art Kreiger's Cigar Factory, it was Flannery's pump that saved the rest of the town. Good thing those Prohibitionists didn't get their way. For more than a century, Flannery's Tavern has been the place to be on St. Patrick's Day.

REALLY OLD

My fourth-grade teacher, Babs Cohen Maza, who grew up in the Harbor and taught school at Washington Elementary in the 1960s, remembers eating at the Indiana Restaurant in the 1930s, which would make it ninety-plus years old. Back then, it was on Fir Street, and you had to order ahead. I tried to find an exact age by calling the restaurant. It had just been sold to a new owner, and no one I talked to could quite figure out how long it had been in business. "But it's old, man," said one of the people who talked to me as the phone was passed around to anyone who might know.

One of the many surprises when writing this book is the number of decades-old restaurants still open. So how do you whittle down which ones to include in the final chapter of this book? All these certainly qualify as classics. But what of the others that remain? Do we count the Home Plate in Hammond even though it's only been open for a little more than thirty years? After all, that's really old for a restaurant. But Region Rats can be very loyal, and there are actually quite a few restaurants in the thirty-year category, so I decided to add another decade as my criteria, focusing on eateries whose doors have been open for forty years or more. In restaurant years, that's like a millennium ago. There are some that won't make this list because I don't know about them, and I apologize for that. But here we go.

During the Great Depression, Harold Miner and Ralph Dunn decided to pool their remaining money—a total of eighty dollars—to open a burger

A true classic, Miner Dunn was founded in 1932. Like Schoop's, another longtime hamburger place that now has numerous locations throughout Northwest Indiana, Miner-Dunn is known for its crisp-edged burgers. *Jill O'Hara, Flickr.*

joint located at 5440 Calumet Avenue in Hammond. Appearance-wise, that first Miner-Dunn was pretty basic—just a tiny kitchen and six stools at the counter. What wasn't basic and what turned it into a knockout Northwest Indiana legacy still going strong after all these years was the winning recipe for hamburgers. The restaurant is now located in Highland and seats more than six but still serves great burgers. Over time, Miner and Dunn expanded their business, opening more restaurants in both Indiana and Illinois.

In 2006, Joe Samara, impressed with the legendary status and delicious taste of Miner-Dunn's hamburgers, which are distinctive because the flattened, griddle-seared patties are crispy edged and juicy and thick in the middle, purchased the restaurant. Determined to keep the name and concept alive as well as to maintain the quality of the food served there, Samara continues the Miner-Dunn's tradition of making "real hamburgers the old-fashioned way."

Dining at Miner-Dunn is like coming home. The atmosphere of the restaurant, which has been located at 8940 Indianapolis Boulevard in Highland for more than sixty years, is cheerful, cozy and friendly. While some restaurants create a retro look, Miner-Dunn is the real deal. The menu still features a great selection of tasty offerings such as meatloaf, French dip sandwiches, Italian beef and chili dogs, house-made soups, delicious pies, hand-spun malts and daily specials.

"We take a lot of pride in using the freshest ingredients, delivering a tried-and-true recipe that has been around since the restaurant first opened," says Samara, noting that they have three to four generations of customers who have been dining at Miner-Dunn for sixty years or more.

The reason? Well, there are several.

"We're still using the same hamburger recipe as Miner and Dunn did when they first opened in 1932," said Samara, who runs the restaurant with his son Ben. "We maintain both the quality and nostalgia."

Indeed, the outdoor sign is still the same, and the restaurant's interior hasn't changed much either—the old-fashioned booths and counters are all part of the charm. Menu items are made from scratch, including their signature orange sherbet; burgers are hand-pressed daily; and the onion rings and French fries are hand-cut.

"We have quite a few people who live out of town and come here on occasion to see family or go to a reunion, and they come in and thank me for keeping the restaurant going the way they remember it," said Samara, who frequently stops by customers' tables to make sure their dining experience was up to expectations.

And here's a secret from those in the know: the ultimate for Miner-Dunn aficionados is to dip the hand-cut fries into the orange sherbet. That, too, is a longtime tradition not to be missed.

Since it opened in 1947, the Town Club in Highland has served more than one and a half million customers for dinners alone, not counting lunches and other meals. And would it surprise you to know that longtime menu offerings include frog legs, boned and buttered perch, southern-style fried chicken, steaks and shrimp cocktail? The restaurant has been described as having the best martini in The Region. The thing is, it's such a winning formula. This is what being classic is all about.

Over 160 years old, the Old Mill Pizzeria and Lounge in Merrillville is the oldest existing structure in town and has managed to survive its time as a dance hall, distillery, candy store, school and—and this is where its name came from—a mill for grinding grain. For almost thirty years it's been a pizzeria and bar.

In 1920, the Brown family brought Valparaiso Home Ice Company, an ice cream store opened by Fred Bartz. Now Valpo Velvet, the ice cream company is still family owned. The Browns have their own formula as well as process for making the seventy-five rich and creamy flavors they sell. Their Valpo Velvet Ice Cream Shoppe also sells sandwiches, soups and salads and features daily specials. A fountain menu is in the collection of the Porter County Museum from the Clover Leaf Dairy, which sold and produced Valpo Velvet ice cream.

In 1941, Gus Romeo opened Flamingo Pizza, an Italian restaurant on Forty-Second and Broadway in Gary and one of the original pizzerias not only in the city but some say the state as well. Over time, the Flamingo would move several times, first to 120 West Fifth Avenue in Gary, where an old handwritten menu shows that baked lasagna cost $1.25, shrimp cocktail $0.75, a large cheese pizza $1.25, Italian beef sandwiches $0.30, a pop $0.10 and the high-ticket price for filet mignon was $1.75. In the 1960s, the Flamingo moved to Forty-Fifth Avenue in Glen Park, and by the mid-1970s, it had relocated again, this time to Miller Beach, where it still is in operation. Though the prices have gone, up they still use the recipes from the original Flamingo, making their own dough, grinding their cheese and mixing their own burgers. "Our steaks are hand cut, the lake perch the real McCoy, we make the original house dressing and nothing is frozen," said owner Willy Lavack.

Baum's Bridge Inn Restaurant and Bar—situated on a bayou formed when the Kankakee River was straightened out, cutting it down from 210 curving miles to an almost yardstick-straight 90 miles—opened in the 1940s,

The Flamingo first opened in Gary in the 1940s. Still in business using the original recipes, it is now located in Miller Beach not far from Lake Michigan. *Andrew Prieboy.*

burned down and then was rebuilt on the same land. Specials include all-you-can-eat walleye or ocean perch, shrimp baskets and tacos. On the regular menu, there are sandwiches like pork tenderloin, ribeye steak, BLT and grilled cheese, as well as hamburgers and pizza.

The Beach Café, just across the street from Flamingo Pizza in the Shelby Beach triangle of Miller Beach, opened in the 1940s. There have been times when it's stood empty, but it's bustling again. New items are added to the menu, but there's boned and buttered perch and frog legs (did you have to ask?), prime rib, burgers, chops, cevapi (a Balkan uncased sausage formed into a patty), sandwiches, seafood and lots of chicken options.

Chuck and Irene Basso opened Chuck and Irene's in 1947 in East Chicago and twelve years later opened a separate location in Hammond. A year later, they decided to sell the East Chicago bar and kept the Hammond business. Chuck and Irene's Bar, Restaurant and Hotel at 6110 Kennedy Avenue is the oldest established business in Hessville, a neighborhood in Hammond's southeast section. Now run by their son Tony, his wife, Geri, and his son Tony, the restaurant remains family owned. Menu items include Chuck's Special Chili, smelt, breaded frog legs, chicken livers and gizzards, tacos, steaks and fried chicken, as well as such specials as lamb on certain Thursdays throughout the year and Italian beef sandwiches.

In his first year in business, Allen Schoop, founder of Schoop's Burgers, sold $2,005 worth of his made-to-order ground beef and hand-formed hamburgers. Though that might not seem like much, consider this. The burgers sold for $0.15 each, and the year was 1948. Adjusted for inflation, that adds up to $22,567.59 in today's money. That's a lot of $0.15 burgers. Now, Schoop's Burgers has sixteen locations through Northwest Indiana and in the Chicagoland area. Forming Schoop Enterprises, the company now has franchises in Nevada and Florida as well as Indiana and Illinois. Schoop's has been voted "Best Hamburger" in the *Times of Northwest Indiana*'s Best of the Region awards since they began over twenty-five years ago.

Since the beginning, Schoop's has been the place to go for fresh ground hamburgers and an array of old-fashioned soda drinks (some of which, like Green River Orange Fanta, weren't old-fashioned back then), floats, shakes, sundaes and scoops of ice cream. Though the hamburgers sell for more than fifteen cents, quality is still paramount.

Dante Zunica opened the House of Pizza in Hammond in 1954. Still family owned, the restaurant is known for its pressed crust and Zunica's special sausage. Now a full-service restaurant, there's also sandwiches; salads; Italian dishes such as lasagna, baked cannelloni, chicken Marsala and that special Chicagoland specialty, Chicken Vesuvio; and, of course, pizza with a long list of toppings, including shrimp, Alfredo sauce, giardiniera and garlic.

Still in business after almost eighty years, the history of the Old Colonial Inn stretches back even further to when it was known as Hotel Kentland. Located on Kentland's old-fashioned courthouse square, it's noticeable because of the tower above the front door. The Colonial Inn's menu is totally classic Northwest Indiana swank—lobster tails, fillets of perch, linguine with clams, prime rib and cocktails such as Golden Cadillacs, Brandy Alexanders, Screwdrivers and Grasshoppers.

As an aside, Fannie W. Hawkins, who took over management of the inn around 1904, somehow garnered some interest by a local reporter who described her work style as "a gadder." Not having any idea what that meant, a Google search was in order. The term, probably more common back in the early 1900s, means to "move about restlessly or with little purpose, especially in search of pleasure or amusement."

You can order other Region-centric fare such as frog legs, perch, fried chicken and roast beef sandwiches at the Cavalier, aka the Cav by those who know this North Hammond neighborhood restaurant opened by Wally Kasprzycki in 1949. But really, it is one of the go-to places for stuffed cabbage, naleśniki (Polish crepes), Polish sausage with sauerkraut, pierogi and Polish potato pancakes. Still family owned, the food is wonderful, but walking in is just as good. It's like entering your Polish grandmother's dining room, albeit if you had a Polish grandmother, but you get the idea. It is very warm and inviting.

The Port Drive-In has been serving home-brewed root beer since opening in Chesterton in 1958. Its long-term motto is "Why drive thru when you can drive in?" Chili dogs, French fries and hamburgers are among the favorites here, and its proximity to the Indiana Dunes National Park makes it a convenient stop.

Freddy's Steakhouse in Hammond has that old-fashioned steak house ambience, the kind of place where you know you're going to get a great meal the moment the server delivers a relish tray and fresh bread with honey butter to the table. This Hammond eatery opened its doors in 1962 and still offers such classics as surf and turf (lobster and filet), perch (of course) and that Chicagoland/Northwest Indiana specialty called saganaki—flaming cheese lit tableside and requiring everyone in the room to shout "opa!" It's a Greek thing, okay? In a surprise move when most everything today is à la carte, soup and salad, in addition to the aforementioned relish tray and bread, come with every meal.

And let's talk about the cocktails. When did you last see a Mai Tai (white rum, dark rum, orange and pineapple juice, grenadine), White Russian (vodka, Kahlua and cream) or Sidecar (brandy, lemon juice and Triple Sec) on a menu that was a for-real old-fashioned place and not a restaurant pretending to be? And who reading this is old enough to have sipped Tia Maria, a coffee liqueur similar to Kahlua but with a more pronounced vanilla taste? Well, they have it here.

Taco Delight on Euclid Avenue in East Chicago also opened in 1962, serving soft and hard tacos (the latter refers to corn tortillas fried and folded over to hold the filling), sopes, burritos, enchiladas, tostados (fried corn tortillas that are served flat and typically topped with refried beans, meat, lettuce, tomato and crumbled Ranchero or Cotija cheese) and tamales, as well as shrimp. Sides are refried beans, Spanish rice and French fries with or without cheese.

Around the same time, the Thumbs Up Tavern in the Miller Beach section of Gary opened its doors. It's a place to drink, but don't worry, the wonderful Miller Beach Pizza is steps away (more about it later).

Since opening in 1966, Giovanni's in Munster has been serving Italian favorites as well as steaks, seafood, chicken and pizzas.

Stanley and Faye Routman opened Zel's on the northwest corner of Euclid and Columbus Avenues in the Indiana Harbor section of East Chicago in 1966. The menu offerings include Nathan's Hot Dogs, corned beef on rye with mustard, chili cheese fries and milkshakes. But the big sellers are the roast beef sandwiches, made with sliced and marinated USDA Choice beef slow cooked for three to four days. Zel's has been so successful that the original restaurants remain, and there are now locations—all painted yellow—throughout Northwest Indiana.

Don's Drive-In in Kentland was initially a Tastee-Freeze but changed its name back in 1974. Carhops and an intercom system create the perfect throw-back to historic drive-ins. If you can't decide what to order, go for the Jumbo Burger.

Offering Lent specials and also keeping up with the times with vegetarian offerings as well as great sandwiches has kept Super Submarine in Hammond in business in 1965.

Madvek's Doghouse opened in 1968, and the menu, with a few additions here and there, has always featured an assortment of Region cuisine, including tacos and American items like French fries. Although it was originally owned by the Madvek family, Mary White bought it over a quarter century ago. It has always featured Vienna all-beef hot dogs and Polish sausages, as well as loose-meat hamburgers. There are a lot of topping choices when it comes to the dogs and sausages—cheese, kraut, chili and chili cheese.

"I've worked for my dad my whole life," Nicolette Skocz said of Rodney D. Langel, who opened his first pizza place in St. John in 1979 before moving two years later to Schererville and opening a store in his hometown of Highland, at 2833 Highway Avenue. Skocz spent her time washing dishes, busing tables, answering phones and, as she tells it, doing "just a little bit of everything." Her dad is still the head honcho, says Skocz. "I still run the business with my dad, and when he does decide to retire, I would like to continue the family business," she said.

Langel's now offers outdoor dining, a large sports bar, two banquet facilities and off-premises catering. Why such success? Skocz mentions friendly staff (the number has grown to more than seventy, from just three at the beginning), as well as the food. "We have one of the best beef sandwiches around, biggest wings, mouth-watering pizza and a delicious ham and cheese hoagie," she said. "We make our own pizza dough, pizza sauce from scratch and utilize fresh ingredients from our produce company." Langel's runs a "pizza of the month," and one of its big hits was "The Big Dill": a dill pickle pizza with a garlic cream base, mozzarella cheese, dill pickles and dill sprinkled on top.

"Growing up, I got to know a lot of the regulars who had been coming in since my dad opened in 1979," said Skocz. "Now I know their kids that are my age that come in regularly. It is a nice feeling to know most of the people that walk through."

Broadway Shrimp in Indiana Harbor opened in the 1980s, and though the city has changed, its specialty—fresh fried shrimp—is still a local favorite.

Dari-Dot opened over a half century ago and has had just two owners since then. "When I bought this twenty-five years ago, it was just a little walk-up window kind of place," said owner Kevin Coppinger, who bought the place rather than be transferred for his corporate job. Business is good. "We serve real ice cream, and we sell 250 to 500 gallons a week."

Established in 1974 by Raymundo and Esther Garcia after a friend complimented her cooking by saying it was good enough to be served in a restaurant, El Taco Real in Hammond is still family owned. Specialties include carne asada (marinated skirt steak) served with Spanish rice, frijoles and a choice of flour or corn tortillas and Pollo Endiablado (one-half chicken sprinkled with paprika, garlic and black pepper and slowly broiled and then topped with a spicy, smoky chipotle sauce). There are also weekly specials, including Pollo Relleno, a chicken breast stuffed with Mexican cheese, onion and tomatoes, dusted with spices and then wrapped in bacon and braised in a chipotle cream sauce.

Tom Gelsosomo, a longtime Italian food aficionado, opened Gelsosomo's Pizza in Portage. Over the years, he would garner awards for best pizza and decided to franchise his winning concept. There are now nine locations: one in Michigan, two in Illinois and the remaining six in Indiana, including his original location.

C&E Donut Shop on Chicago Avenue and Alexander Street in the Calumet section of East Chicago is still serving donuts as well as sandwiches and burgers since opening in the 1940s.

Johnsen's Blue Top Drive-In on Indianapolis Boulevard in Highland is a long way from Southern California, where the Googie style of architecture got its start. If you've ever seen *The Jetsons*, a popular television series from the early 1960s, you'll understand the look—very jet age modern (or what was thought to be jet age modern) defined by bold signage, inverted triangles, glass walls and off-kilter angles. An offshoot of the Streamline Moderne architecture of the 1930s, it evolved just a little later that same decade and lasted until the mid- to late 1960s.

Johnsen's Blue Top Drive-In, a classic diner from the mid-twentieth century, with muscle cars and carhops. *Flickr*.

Well, when it comes to Googie in Indiana, Johnsen's Blue Top (the name refers to the roof of the original restaurant at the same location), built in 1964 and still in business, is considered one of the best examples of that architectural style. And for good reason: it's distinctive, with a roof canopy designed to look like a folded plate, inverted rooflines and a twenty-eight-foot-tall neon sign.

In contrast to the space age, in 1912, Americao Joseph Semento was definitely old country when he emigrated from Provincia di Avellino in the Campania region of Italy to Chicago, where he worked as a tailor. He moved his shop to Valparaiso eight years later. In 1939, Mike (as he was called) and his wife, Teresa, built the Semento Napoli Café on a main dirt road in Valparaiso. At the time, looking at old photos, it appeared to be in the middle of nowhere, but the Sementos figured that with the opening of the Lincoln Highway, a transcontinental thoroughfare that is now U.S. 30, it would soon be a busy place, and they were right.

Living in the back of the restaurant, Mike raised vegetables and displayed them behind the bar. Still in the family, it is a fourth-generation restaurant and one of the oldest in business in Valparaiso.

The Calumet Tap on Kennedy Avenue and 150th sometimes was nicknamed the "Bucket of Blood" because of the fights and sometimes worse that took place there, but it's been open since at least the 1950s, so people must enjoy the food and drinks and maybe the excitement.

In 1977, Manuel Tellez, nicknamed Papa Man, opened Casa Blanca Restaurant on Indianapolis Avenue in East Chicago. An elaborate place, stepping through its doors transposes one from the grim environs of Indianapolis Boulevard into a Spanish courtyard with flowing fountains, tiled walls and floor and arched entranceways into the different rooms. Though sadly Manuel passed away a few years ago, Casa Blanca remains open, and family recipes are still followed in making the popular dishes. It's a large place, capable of seating two hundred at its tables and booths covered with pink tablecloths.

The menu, based on recipes like those made in Mexican homes, lists Carne Tampiquena or carne asada served with enchiladas, Huachinago Entero (whole red snapper in a garlic butter sauce), Camarones Thermado (shrimp with mushroom cooked in cream and cherry wine), tacos and burritos and Queso Fundido Caserola. The bar serves up sangria, margaritas, piña coladas, Tequila Sunrises, Tequila Sours and daiquiris.

Arman's in Miller Beach has been selling sandwiches such as Polish sausage (get it with relish and onions), Italian beef, Vienna hot dogs and shoestring fried potatoes for sixty-five years or so.

Gary and Scott Goldberg, a father-son who were from the Chicago suburbs, opened Miller Beach Pizza (MBP) in downtown Miller in 1985, focusing on serving the food they'd grown up eating, including—besides pizza—homemade Italian sandwiches and other sandwiches such as Italian sausage and strombolis. Their pizza includes thin crust (which is cut in the Northwest Indiana way, into squares and triangles), deep dish and stuffed and includes the typical toppings as well as such specialties as gyros and Italian beef. Still a family place, MBP is owned by Gary and Elsie Goldberg.

Also in 1985, Carlos Rivero opened the first Spanish restaurant in the state at a time when the term *tapas* was known only to international travelers. Since then, his restaurant, Don Quijote, has been serving authentic Spanish cuisine, including paellas, tapas or small plates and house-made sangria.

George's Family Restaurant in Lowell opened in 1986 as a family-friendly, family-style eatery serving classic American food with some Greek and Mexican additions on the menu as well, such as their Greek yogurt and Greek omelet and their Despacito Burrito—scrambled eggs, chorizo, onions and cheddar cheese wrapped in a pressed flour tortilla and topped with sour cream, guacamole and cilantro or homemade chorizo. There are also American classics like country fried steak and eggs.

Though Meyer's Castle has been a restaurant for just a little over thirty years, I thought it was necessary to include it. After all, it is a castle—or at least a replica of one that the original owner liked when visiting Scotland and had built in 1929. And yes, seeing it leaves no doubt that this massive castle built of Indiana limestone in an elaborate style known as Jacobethan Revival, featuring multi-curved Flemish gables, Tudor arches, casement windows and decorative chimneys, is as close to a castle as one will find in Northwest Indiana. When Sergio and Elizabeth Urquiza bought the twenty-eight-room Meyer's Castle in 1987 as a home, they quickly realized it was too big just to live in, so they turned it into a restaurant as well.

THE CHAMP

Finally, there's Teibel's in Schererville, which opened in 1929 as a twelve-seat roadside diner and within a decade was earning kudos as one of the best restaurants with great service and dining. Half of a fried chicken sold for sixty-five cents.

"My father, Steve, started working at Teibel's in the late '70s," said Paul Teibel. "He took over for his father and grandfather, Harold and Stephen. I began working at Teibel's in 2005 and am currently raising the fifth generation."

Schererville was a sleepy little town when the restaurant first opened. Indeed, the number of people living there, as recorded by the U.S. census the following year, was 580, but its location was great. It was at the intersection of U.S. Highways 30 and 41 that has been a regional crossroads for centuries, dating to when Native Americans from the Pottawatomie, Fox and several other tribes traversed the area.

It was even smaller, having been founded by German immigrants, when, according to a newspaper article, Michael Seberger, whose father settled in the area in 1842, recalled that his dad had chickens that slept in the trees at night. When the weather was very cold, they would freeze to death and fall to the ground.

It was almost a daily routine over forty years ago for Butch Grimmer and Steve Teibel to wave to each other on their way to work. Grimmer was working for Grimmer's Service (the family auto repair business his father started after returning from World War II) and deciding he didn't want to work in the steel mills, and Teibel was on his way to the restaurant his family had founded in 1929. Their businesses were just doors apart. "Now my son Brian waves at his son Paul as they pass each other on the way to work," said Grimmer.

"It's neat to occasionally think about being part of our town's history," said Teibel. "Some great families have made our town a special place and strong community. Family-owned businesses filled with hardworking relatives have always been the rock of the local economy. Buying local is and has been a focal point for Teibel's since Stephen and Marty opened up shop in 1929. When we walk through our dining rooms, we always see other local business owners and employees whom we have formed strong friendships and business relationships with."

About the Author

Ever since she started her own newspaper at age eight and sold it to neighbors who had no choice but to subscribe, Jane Simon Ammeson has loved to write. She's now upped her game, writing about travel, food and history for newspapers, magazines and websites. She has also authored fifteen books, and her *Lincoln Road Trip: Back-Roads Guide to America's Favorite President* was a winner in the 2019–20 Lowell Thomas Travel Journalism Competition, taking the bronze in the Travel Book category. A graduate of Indiana University, Jane lives in Southwest Michigan.

Visit us at
www.historypress.com